Node Web Development

A practical introduction to Node, the exciting new
server-side JavaScript web development stack

D1571642

David Herron

PUBLISHING

BIRMINGHAM - MUMBAI

Node Web Development

First published: August 2011

Production Reference: 1020811

Published by Packt Publishing Ltd.
Livery Place
35 Livery Street
Birmingham B3 2PB, UK.

ISBN 978-1-849515-14-6

www.packtpub.com

Cover Image by David Lorenz Winston (david@davidlorenzwinston.com)

Credits

Author
David Herron

Reviewers
Blagovest Dachev

Matt Ranney

Acquisition Editor
Sarah Cullington

Development Editor
Pallavi Iyengar

Technical Editor
Joyslita D'Souza

Project Coordinator
Joel Goveya

Proofreader
Aaron Nash

Indexers
Hemangini Bari

Tejal Daruwale

Production Coordinator
Alwin Roy

Cover Work
Alwin Roy

About the Author

David Herron has worked in the software industry, holding both developer and quality engineering roles, in Silicon Valley for over 20 years. His most recent role was at Yahoo! as an Architect of the Quality Engineering team for their new Node-based web application platform.

While a Staff Engineer at Sun Microsystems, David worked as an Architect of the Java SE Quality Engineering team, where he focused on test automation tools, including the AWT Robot class that's now widely used in GUI test automation software. He was involved with launching the OpenJDK project, the JDK-Distros project, and ran the worldwide Mustang Regressions Contest asking the Java developer community to find bugs in the Java 1.6 release.

Before Sun, he worked for VXtreme on the video streaming stack, which eventually became Windows Media Player when Microsoft bought that company. At The Wollongong Group, he worked on both e-mail client and server software and was part of several IETF working groups improving e-mail-related protocols.

David is interested in electric vehicles, world energy supplies, climate change, and environmental issues, and is a co-founder of Transition Silicon Valley. As an online journalist on examiner.com he writes under the title Green Transportation Examiner, he blogs about sustainability issues on 7gen.com, runs a large electric vehicle discussion website on visforvoltage.org, and blogs about other topics including Node.js, Drupal, and Doctor Who on davidherron.com.

Acknowledgement

There are many people I am grateful to.

I wish to thank my mother, Evelyn, for, well everything; my father, Jim; my sister, Patti; and my brother, Ken. What would life be without all of you?

I wish to thank my girlfriend, Maggie, for being there and encouraging me, her belief in me, her wisdom and humor, and kicks in the butt when needed. May we have many more years of this.

I wish to thank Dr. Ken Kubota of the University of Kentucky, for believing in me, and giving me my first job in computing. It was six years of learning not just the art of computer system maintenance, but so much more.

I wish to thank my former employers, University of Kentucky Mathematical Sciences Department, The Wollongong Group, MainSoft, VXtreme, Sun Microsystems, and Yahoo!, and all the people I worked with in each company. I am grateful to my ex-manager Tina Su, who kept pushing me towards public speaking and writing, neither of which are natural for an introvert software engineer. I am especially grateful to Yahoo, for giving me an opportunity to work on their internal Node.js effort, and to accommodate the needs of writing this book.

I am grateful to Packt Publishing for giving me this opportunity to write a book, for making me realize that my dream is to write books, and for their expert guidance through the process.

I am grateful to Ryan Dahl, Isaac Schlueter, and the other Node core team members for having the wisdom and vision needed to create such a joy-filled fluid software development platform. Some platforms are just plain hard to work with, but not this one, and that takes vision to implement it so well.

About the Reviewers

Blagovest Dachev has been writing software for the Web since 2002. He went through the full spectrum of development by starting out with HTML, CSS, and JavaScript, then moving into the server and database world. Blagovest was an early adopter of Node.js and had contributed to several open source projects. He is currently a software engineer for Dow Jones & Company, where he works on a widget framework allowing third parties to search and display news on their websites.

Blagovest attended the University of Massachusetts at Amherst where he participated in information retrieval research, completed two consecutive Google Summer of Code mandates, and co-authored several papers.

> I would like to thank my mother Tatiana for her love, relentless devotion, and strength, which has inspired me through the years, and my father Jordan for all the happy memories from my childhood.

Matt Ranney is an early adopter and contributor to Node.js. He is one of the founders of Voxer, which uses Node on its backend servers.

www.PacktPub.com

Support files, eBooks, discount offers and more

You might want to visit www.PacktPub.com for support files and downloads related to your book.

Did you know that Packt offers eBook versions of every book published, with PDF and ePub files available? You can upgrade to the eBook version at www.PacktPub.com and as a print book customer, you are entitled to a discount on the eBook copy. Get in touch with us at service@packtpub.com for more details.

At www.PacktPub.com, you can also read a collection of free technical articles, sign up for a range of free newsletters and receive exclusive discounts and offers on Packt books and eBooks.

http://PacktLib.PacktPub.com

Do you need instant solutions to your IT questions? PacktLib is Packt"s online digital book library. Here, you can access, read and search across Packt"s entire library of books.

Why Subscribe?

- Fully searchable across every book published by Packt
- Copy and paste, print and bookmark content
- On demand and accessible via web browser

Free Access for Packt account holders

If you have an account with Packt at www.PacktPub.com, you can use this to access PacktLib today and view nine entirely free books. Simply use your login credentials for immediate access.

Table of Contents

Preface

Welcome to the world of developing web software using Node (also known as Node. js). Node is a newly-developed software platform that liberates JavaScript from the web browser, enabling it to be used as a general software development platform in server-side applications. It runs atop the ultra-fast JavaScript engine from the Chrome browser, V8, and adds in a fast and robust library of asynchronous network I/O modules. The primary focus of Node is on building high performance, highly scalable server and client applications for the "Real Time Web".

The platform was developed by Ryan Dahl in 2009 after a couple of years of experimenting with developing web server components in Ruby and other languages. The exploration led him to the architectural choice of using asynchronous event-driven systems rather than the traditional thread-based concurrency model. This model was chosen because it's simpler (threaded systems are notoriously difficult to develop), has lower overhead over maintaining a thread-per-connection, and for speed. The goal of Node is to provide an "easy way to build scalable network servers". The design is similar to and influenced by other systems such as Event Machine (Ruby) and Twisted framework (Python).

This book, Node Web Development, focuses on building web applications using Node. We will be taking a tour through the important concepts required to speed up with Node. To do so we'll be writing real applications, dissecting them to scrutinize how they work, and discussing how to apply the ideas to your own programs. We'll install Node and npm, and learn how to install or develop npm packages and Node modules. We'll develop several applications, ponder the effects of long-running calculations on event loop responsiveness, look at a couple of ways to distribute heavy workloads to other servers, work with the Express framework, and more.

What this book covers

Chapter 1, What is Node?, introduces you to the Node platform. We cover its uses, the technological architectural choices in Node, its history, and the history of server-side JavaScript, and why JavaScript should remain trapped in browsers.

Chapter 2, Setting up Node, goes over setting up a Node developer environment, including several scenarios of compiling and installing from source code. We briefly touch on Node deployment to production servers.

Chapter 3, Node Modules, explains that modules are the unit of modularity in developing Node applications. We take a dive into understanding and developing Node modules. We then take a close look at npm, the Node Package Manager, and several scenarios using npm to manage installed packages, or to develop npm packages and distribute them for others.

Chapter 4, Variations on a Simple Application, explains that with the fundamentals in hand we begin exploring application development in Node. Specifically we develop a simple application using Node itself, the Connect middleware framework, and the Express application framework. While the application is simple, it gives us a chance to explore the Node event loop, accommodating long running calculations, asynchronous and synchronous algorithms, and pushing heavy calculations to a backend server.

Chapter 5, A Simple Web Server, EventEmitters, and HTTP Clients, explains that in Node the HTTP client and server objects are front and center. We take a close look at both ends of the HTTP conversation by developing both HTTP client and server applications.

Chapter 6, Data Storage and Retrieval, explains that most applications need some sort of long-term reliable data storage. We look at implementing an application with both SQL and MongoDB database engines. Along the way we cover user authentication and presenting a better error page, using the Express framework.

What you need for this book

Today, we normally install Node from source, and it works best on Unix- or POSIX-like systems. The requirements to begin using Node are modest, and your most important tool is the one between your ears.

Installing from source requires a Unix-/POSIX-like system (Linux, Mac, FreeBSD, OpenSolaris, and so on), modern C/C++ compiler, the OpenSSL libraries, and Python version 2.4 or later.

Node programs can be edited with any text editor, but one that can handle JavaScript, HTML, CSS, and so on will be useful.

While the book is about developing web applications, it does not require you to have a web server. Node provides its own web server stack.

Who this book is for

This book was written for any software engineer who wants the adventure that comes with a new software platform embodying a new programming paradigm.

Server-side engineers may find the concepts refreshing, giving you a different perspective on web application development. JavaScript is a powerful language and Node's asynchronous nature plays to JavaScript's strengths.

Developers experienced with JavaScript in the browser may find it fun to bring that knowledge to a new territory, and to write in JavaScript without accessing the DOM. (There's no browser, hence no DOM, unless you install JSDom.)

While the chapters build on each other, how you read this book is up to you.

We assume you already know how to write software, and have an understanding of modern programming languages such as JavaScript.

Conventions

In this book, you will find a number of styles of text that distinguish between different kinds of information. Here are some examples of these styles, and an explanation of their meaning.

Code words in text are shown as follows: "The `http` object encapsulates the HTTP protocol and its `http.createServer` method creates a whole web server, listening on the port specified in the `.listen` method."

A block of code is set as follows:

```
var http = require('http');
http.createServer(function (req, res) {
  res.writeHead(200, {'Content-Type': 'text/plain'});
  res.end('Hello World\n');
}).listen(8124, "127.0.0.1");
console.log('Server running at http://127.0.0.1:8124/');
```

When we wish to draw your attention to a particular part of a code block, the relevant lines or items are set in bold:

```
var util = require('util');
var A = "a different value A";
```

```
var B = "a different value B";
var m1 = require('./module1');
util.log('A='+A+' B='+B+' values='+util.inspect(m1.values()));
```

Any command-line input or output is written as follows:

```
$ sudo /usr/sbin/update-rc.d node defaults
```

New terms and **important words** are shown in bold. Words that you see on the screen, in menus or dialog boxes for example, appear in the text like this: "A real security system would have fields for at least a username and password. Instead we'll skip this and just ask the user to click the **Login** button."

Reader feedback

Feedback from our readers is always welcome. Let us know what you think about this book—what you liked or may have disliked. Reader feedback is important for us to develop titles that you really get the most out of.

To send us general feedback, simply send an e-mail to feedback@packtpub.com, and mention the book title via the subject of your message.

If there is a book that you need and would like to see us publish, please send us a note in the **SUGGEST A TITLE** form on www.packtpub.com or e-mail suggest@packtpub.com.

If there is a topic that you have expertise in and you are interested in either writing or contributing to a book, see our author guide on www.packtpub.com/authors.

Customer support

Now that you are the proud owner of a Packt book, we have a number of things to help you to get the most from your purchase.

Downloading the example code

You can download the example code files for all Packt books you have purchased from your account at http://www.PacktPub.com. If you purchased this book elsewhere, you can visit http://www.PacktPub.com/support and register to have the files e-mailed directly to you.

Errata

Although we have taken every care to ensure the accuracy of our content, mistakes do happen. If you find a mistake in one of our books—maybe a mistake in the text or the code—we would be grateful if you would report this to us. By doing so, you can save other readers from frustration and help us improve subsequent versions of this book. If you find any errata, please report them by visiting `http://www.packtpub.com/support`, selecting your book, clicking on the **errata submission form** link, and entering the details of your errata. Once your errata are verified, your submission will be accepted and the errata will be uploaded on our website, or added to any list of existing errata, under the Errata section of that title. Any existing errata can be viewed by selecting your title from `http://www.packtpub.com/support`.

Piracy

Piracy of copyright material on the Internet is an ongoing problem across all media. At Packt, we take the protection of our copyright and licenses very seriously. If you come across any illegal copies of our works, in any form, on the Internet, please provide us with the location address or website name immediately so that we can pursue a remedy.

Please contact us at copyright@packtpub.com with a link to the suspected pirated material.

We appreciate your help in protecting our authors, and our ability to bring you valuable content.

Questions

You can contact us at `questions@packtpub.com` if you are having a problem with any aspect of the book, and we will do our best to address it.

1
What is Node?

Node is an exciting new platform for developing web applications, application servers, any sort of network server or client, and general purpose programming. It is designed for extreme scalability in networked applications through an ingenious combination of asynchronous I/O, server-side JavaScript, smart use of JavaScript anonymous functions, and a single execution thread event-driven architecture.

The Node model is very different from common application server platforms that scale using threads. The claim is that, because of the event-driven architecture, memory footprint is low, throughput is high, and the programming model is simpler. The Node platform is in a phase of rapid growth, and many are seeing it as a compelling alternative to the traditional—Apache, PHP, Python, and so on—approach to building web applications.

At heart it is a standalone JavaScript virtual machine, with extensions making it suitable for general purpose programming, and with a clear focus on application server development. The Node platform isn't directly comparable to programming languages frequently used for developing web applications (PHP/Python/Ruby/Java/ and so on), neither is it directly comparable to the containers which deliver the HTTP protocol to web clients (Apache/Tomcat/Glassfish/ and so on). At the same time, many regard it as potentially supplanting the traditional web applications development stacks.

It is implemented around a non-blocking I/O event loop and a layer of file and network I/O libraries, all built on top of the V8 JavaScript engine (from the Chrome web browser). The I/O library is general enough to implement any sort of server implementing any TCP or UDP protocol, whether it's DNS, HTTP, IRC, FTP, and so on. While it supports developing servers or clients for any network protocol, the biggest use case is regular websites where you're replacing things like an Apache/PHP or Rails stack.

This book will give you an introduction to Node. We presume that you already know how to write software, are familiar with JavaScript, and know something about developing web applications in other languages. We will dive right into developing working applications and recognize that often the best way to learn is by rummaging around in working code.

What can you do with Node?

Node is a platform for writing JavaScript applications outside web browsers. This is not the JavaScript we are familiar with in web browsers. There is no DOM built into Node, nor any other browser capability. With the JavaScript language and the asynchronous I/O framework, it is a powerful application development platform.

One thing Node cannot do is desktop GUI applications. Today, there is no equivalent for Swing (or SWT if you prefer) built into Node, nor is there a Node add-on GUI toolkit, nor can it be embedded in a web browser. If a GUI toolkit were available Node could be used to build desktop applications. Some projects have begun to create GTK bindings for Node, which would provide a cross-platform GUI toolkit. The V8 engine used by Node brings along with it an extension API, allowing one to incorporate C/C++ code, to extend JavaScript or to integrate with native code libraries.

Beyond its native ability to execute JavaScript, the bundled modules provide capabilities of this sort:

- Command-line tools (in shell script style)
- Interactive-TTY style of program (REPL or Read-Eval-Print Loop)
- Excellent process control functions to oversee child processes
- A Buffer object to deal with binary data
- TCP or UDP sockets with comprehensive event driven callbacks
- DNS lookup
- Layered on top of the TCP library is a HTTP and HTTPS client/server
- File system access
- Built-in rudimentary unit testing support through assertions

The network layer of Node is low level while being simple to use. For example, the HTTP modules allow you to write an HTTP server (or client) in a few lines of code, but that layer puts you, the programmer, very close to the protocol requests and makes you implement precisely which HTTP headers will be returned in responding to requests. Where a PHP programmer generally doesn't care about the headers, a Node programmer does.

In other words, it's very easy to write an HTTP server in Node, but the typical web application developer doesn't need to work at that level of detail. For example, PHP coders assume Apache is already there, and that they don't have to implement the HTTP server portion of the stack. The Node community has developed a wide range of web application frameworks like Connect, allowing developers to quickly configure an HTTP server that provides all of the basics we've come to expect— sessions, cookies, serving static files, logging, and so on—thus letting developers focus on their business logic.

Server-side JavaScript

Quit scratching your head already. Of course you're doing it, scratching your head and mumbling to yourself, "What's a browser language doing on the server?" In truth, JavaScript has a long and largely unknown history outside the browser. JavaScript is a programming language, just like any other language, and the better question to ask is "Why should JavaScript remain trapped inside browsers?"

Back in the dawn of the Web age, the tools for writing web applications were at a fledgling stage. Some were experimenting with Perl or TCL to write CGI scripts, the PHP and Java languages had just been developed, and even JavaScript was being used in the server side. One early web application server was Netscape's LiveWire server, which used JavaScript. Some versions of Microsoft's ASP used JScript, their version of JavaScript. A more recent server-side JavaScript project is the RingoJS application framework in the Java universe. It is built on top of Rhino, a JavaScript implementation written in Java.

Node brings to the table a combination never seen before. Namely, the coupling of fast event-driven I/O and a fast JavaScript engine like V8, the ultra fast JavaScript engine at the heart of Google's Chrome web browser.

Why should you use Node?

The JavaScript language is very popular due to its ubiquity in web browsers. It compares favorably against other languages while having many modern advanced language concepts. Thanks to its popularity there is a deep talent pool of experienced JavaScript programmers out there.

It is a dynamic programming language with loosely typed and dynamically extendable objects, that can be informally declared as needed. Functions are a first class object routinely used as anonymous closures. This makes JavaScript more powerful than some other languages commonly used for web applications. In theory these features make developers more productive. To be fair, the debate between dynamic and non-dynamic languages, or between statically typed and loosely typed, is not settled and may never be settled.

One of the main disadvantages of JavaScript is the Global Object. All of the top-level variables are tossed together in the Global Object, which can create an unruly chaos when mixing modules together. Since web applications tend to have lot of objects, probably coded by multiple organizations, one may think programming in Node will be a minefield of conflicting global objects. Instead, Node uses the CommonJS module system, meaning that variables local to a module are truly local to the module, even if they look like global variables. This clean separation between modules prevents the Global Object problem from being a problem.

Having the same programming language on server and client has been a long-time dream on the Web. This dream dates back to the early days of Java, where Applets were to be the frontend to server applications written in Java, and JavaScript was originally envisioned as a lightweight scripting language for Applets. Something fell down along the way, and we ended up with JavaScript as the principle in browser client-side language, rather than Java. With Node we may finally be able to implement that dream of the same programming language on client and server, with JavaScript at both ends of the Web, in the browser and server.

A common language for frontend and backend offers several potential wins:

- The same programming staff can work on both ends of the wire
- Code can be migrated between server and client more easily
- Common data formats (JSON) between server and client
- Common software tools for server and client
- Common testing or quality reporting tools for server and client
- When writing web applications, view templates can be used on both sides
- Similar languaging between server and client teams

Node facilitates implementing all these positive benefits (and more) with a compelling platform and development community.

Architecture: Threads versus asynchronous event-driven

The asynchronous event-driven architecture of Node is said to be the cause of its blistering performance. Well, that and the V8 JavaScript engine. The normal application server model uses blocking I/O and threads for concurrency. Blocking I/O causes threads to wait, causing churn between threads as they are forced to wait on I/O while the application server handles requests.

Node has a single execution thread with no waiting on I/O or context switching. Instead, I/O calls set up request handling functions that work with the event loop to dispatch events when some things becomes available. The event loop and event handler model is common, such as JavaScript execution in a web browser. Program execution is expected to quickly return to the event loop for dispatching the next immediately runnable task.

To help us wrap our heads around this, Ryan Dahl (in his *"Cinco de Node"* presentation) asked us what happens while executing a code like this:

```
result = query('SELECT * from db');
```

Of course, the program pauses at that point while the database layer sends the query to the database, which determines the result, and returns the data. Depending on the query that pause can be quite long. This is bad because while the entire thread is idling another request might come in, and if all the threads are busy (remember computers have finite resources) it will be dropped. Looks like quite a waste. Context switching is not free either, the more threads we use the more time the CPU spends in storing and restoring the state. Furthermore, the execution stack for each thread takes up memory. Simply by using asynchronous, event-driven I/O, Node removes most of this overhead while introducing very little on its own.

Frequently the implementation of concurrency with threads comes with admonitions like these: "expensive and error-prone", "the error-prone synchronization primitives of Java", or "designing concurrent software can be complex and error-prone" (actual quotes from actual search engine results). The complexity comes from the access to shared variables and various strategies to avoid deadlock and competition between threads. The "synchronization primitives of Java" are an example of such a strategy, and obviously many programmers find them hard to use; and then there's the tendency to create frameworks like `java.util.concurrent` to tame the complexity of threaded concurrency, but some might argue that papering over complexity does not make things simpler.

Node asks us to think differently about concurrency. Callbacks fired asynchronously from an event loop are a much simpler concurrency model, simpler to understand, and simpler to implement.

Ryan Dahl points to the relative access time of objects to understand the need for asynchronous I/O. Objects in memory are more quickly accessed (on the order of nanoseconds) than objects on disk or objects retrieved over the network (milliseconds or seconds). The longer access time for external objects is measured in the zillions of clock cycles, which can be an eternity when your customer is sitting at their web browser ready to be bored and move on if it takes longer than two seconds to load the page.

In Node, the query discussed previously would read like the following:

```
query('SELECT * from db', function (result) {
  // operate on result
});
```

This code makes the same query written earlier. The difference is that the query result is not the result of the function call, but is provided to a callback function that will be called later. What happens is that this will return almost immediately to the event loop, and the server can go on to servicing other requests. One of those requests will be the response to the query and it will invoke the callback function. This model of quickly returning to the event loop ensures higher server utilization. That's great for the owner of the server, but there's an even bigger gain which might help the user to experience more quickly constructing page content.

Commonly web pages bring together data from dozens of sources. Each one has a query and response as discussed earlier. By using asynchronous queries each one can happen in parallel, where the page construction function can fire off dozens of queries — no waiting, each with their own callback — then go back to the event loop, invoking the callbacks as each is done. Because it's in parallel the data can be collected much more quickly than if these queries were done synchronously one at a time. Now the reader on their web browser is happier because the page loads more quickly.

Performance and utilization

Some of the excitement over Node is due to its throughput (requests per second it can serve). Comparative benchmarks of similar applications, for example, Apache and Node, show it having tremendous performance gains.

One benchmark going around is this simple HTTP server, which simply returns a "Hello World" message, directly from memory:

```
var http = require('http');
http.createServer(function (req, res) {
  res.writeHead(200, {'Content-Type': 'text/plain'});
  res.end('Hello World\n');
}).listen(8124, "127.0.0.1");
console.log('Server running at http://127.0.0.1:8124/');
```

This is one of the simpler web servers one can build with Node. The `http` object encapsulates the HTTP protocol and its `http.createServer` method creates a whole web server, listening on the port specified in the `.listen` method. Every request (whether a GET or PUT on any URL) on that web server calls the provided function. It is very simple and lightweight. In this case, regardless of the URL, it returns a simple `text/plain` "**Hello World**" response.

Because of its minimal nature, this simple application should demonstrate the maximum request throughput of Node. Indeed many have published benchmark studies starting from this simplest of HTTP servers.

Ryan Dahl (Node's original author) showed a simple benchmark (`http://nodejs.org/cinco_de_node.pdf`) which returned a 1 megabyte binary buffer; Node gave 822 req/sec, while nginx gave 708 req/sec. He also noted that nginx peaked at 4 megabytes memory, while Node peaked at 64 megabytes.

Dustin McQuay (`http://www.synchrosinteractive.com/blog/9-nodejs/22-nodejs-has-a-bright-future`) showed what he claimed were similar Node and PHP/Apache programs:

- PHP/Apache 3187 requests/second
- Node.js 5569 requests/second

Hannes Wallnöfer, the author of RingoJS, wrote a blog post in which he cautioned against making important decisions based on benchmarks (`http://hns.github.com/2010/09/21/benchmark.html`), and then went on to use benchmarks to compare RingoJS with Node. RingoJS is an app server built around the Rhino JavaScript engine for Java. Depending on the scenario, the performance of RingoJS and Node is not so far apart. The findings show that on applications with rapid buffer or string allocation, Node performs worse than RingoJS. In a later blog post (`http://hns.github.com/2010/09/29/benchmark2.html`) he used a JSON string parsing workload to simulate a common task, and found RingoJS to be much better.

Mikito Takada blogged about benchmarking and performance improvements in a "48 hour hackathon" application he built (`http://blog.mixu.net/2011/01/17/performance-benchmarking-the-node-js-backend-of-our-48h-product-wehearvoices-net/`) comparing Node with what he claims is a similar application written with Django. The unoptimized Node version is quite a bit slower (response time) than the Django version but a few optimizations (MySQL connection pooling, caching, and so on) made drastic performance improvements handily beating out Django. The final performance graph shows achieving nearly the requests/second rate of the simple "Hello World" benchmark discussed earlier.

A key realization about Node performance is the need to quickly return to the event loop. We go over this in *Chapter 4, Variations on a Simple Application* in more detail, but if a callback handler takes "too long" to execute, it will prevent Node from being the blistering fast server it was designed to be. In one of Ryan Dahl's earliest blog posts about the Node project (`http://four.livejournal.com/963421.html`) he discussed a requirement that event handlers execute within 5ms. Most of the ideas in that post were never implemented, but Alex Payne wrote an intriguing blog post on this, (`http://al3x.net/2010/07/27/node.html`) drawing a distinction between "scaling in the small" and "scaling in the large".

Small-scale web applications (*"scaling in the small"*) should have performance and implementation advantages when written for Node instead of the 'P' languages (Perl, PHP, Python, and so on) normally used. JavaScript is a powerful language, and the Node environment with its modern fast virtual machine design offers performance and concurrency advantages over interpreted languages like PHP.

He goes on to argue that *"scaling in the large"*, enterprise-level applications, will always be hard and complex. One typically throws in load balancers, caching servers, multiple redundant machines, in geographically dispersed locations, to serve zillions of users from around the world with a fast web browsing experience. Perhaps the application development platform isn't so important as the whole system.

We won't know how well Node really fits in until it sees real long-term deployment in significant production environments.

Server utilization, the bottom line, and green web hosting

The striving for optimal efficiency (handling more requests/second) is not just about the geeky satisfaction that comes from optimization. There are real business and environmental benefits. Handling more requests per second, as Node servers can do, means the difference between buying lots of servers and buying only a few servers. Essentially the advantage is in doing more with less.

Roughly speaking, the more servers one buys, the greater the cost, and the greater the environmental impact, and likewise buying fewer servers means lower cost and lower environmental impact. There's a whole field of expertise around reducing cost and environmental impact of running web server facilities, which that rough guideline doesn't do justice to. The goal is fairly obvious, fewer servers, lower costs, and lower environmental impact.

Intel's paper *"Increasing Data Center Efficiency with Server Power Measurements"* (http://download.intel.com/it/pdf/Server_Power_Measurement_final. pdf) gives an objective framework for understanding efficiency and data center costs. There are many factors such as building, cooling system, and computer system design. Efficient building design, efficient cooling systems, and efficient computer systems (Datacenter Efficiency, Datacenter Density, and Storage Density) can decrease costs and environmental impact. But you can destroy those gains by deploying an inefficient software stack which compels you to buy more servers than if you had an efficient software stack, or you can amplify gains from datacenter efficiency with an efficient software stack.

Spelling: Node, Node.js, or Node.JS?

The name of the platform is Node.js but throughout this book we are spelling it as Node because we are following a cue from the `nodejs.org` website, which says the trademark is Node.js (lower case `.js`) but throughout the site they spell it as Node. We are doing the same in this book.

Summary

We've learned a lot in this chapter, specifically:

- That JavaScript has a life outside web browsers
- The difference between asynchronous and blocking I/O
- A look at Node
- Node performance

Now that we've had this introduction to Node we're ready to dive in and start using it. In *Chapter 2, Setting up Node* we'll go over setting up a Node environment, so let's get started.

2
Setting up Node

Before getting started with using Node you must set up your development environment. In the following chapters we'll be using this for development, and for non-production deployment.

In this chapter we shall:

- See how to install Node from source on Linux or Mac
- See how to install the npm package manager, and some popular tools
- Learn a bit about the Node module system

So let's get on with it.

System requirements

Node runs best on the POSIX-like operating systems. These are the various UNIX derivatives (Solaris, and so on) or workalikes (Linux, Mac OS X, and so on). Indeed many of the Node built-in functions are direct corollaries to POSIX system calls.

More mature language platforms (such as Perl or Python) have a stable feature set and API and are routinely bundled into operating system distributions. Since Node is still in rapid development, it would be premature for OS distributions to prepackage binary builds of Node. This means the preferred method is to install Node from the source.

Installing from source requires having a C compiler (such as GCC), and Python 2.4 (or later). If you plan to use encryption in your networking code you will also need the OpenSSL cryptographic library. The modern UNIX derivatives almost certainly come with these, and Node's configure script (see later when we download and configure the source) will detect their presence. If you should have to install them, Python is available at `http://python.org` and OpenSSL is at `http://openssl.org`.

While Windows is not POSIX compatible, Node can be built on it either using POSIX compatibility environments (in Node 0.4.x and earlier). In 0.6.x and later, the Node team intends for it to be buildable natively on Windows. The instructions for building Node on Windows is changing too rapidly to print in a book, and up-to-date instructions are at https://github.com/ry/node/wiki/Installation. Step 3b discusses building on Windows using either Cygwin or MinGW. The steps, once either Cygwin or MinGW is installed, are similar to the ones for POSIX-like systems.

Installation on POSIX-like systems (Linux, Solaris, Mac, and so on)

Now that you have the high-level view, let's get our hands dirty mucking around in some build scripts. The general process follows the usual configure, make, make install routine that you may already have performed with other software.

The official installation instructions are in the Node wiki at:

https://github.com/ry/node/wiki/Installation

Installing prerequisites

As noted a minute ago there are three prerequisites, a C compiler, Python, and the OpenSSL libraries. The Node installation process checks for their presence and will fail if the C compiler or Python is not present. The specific method of installing these is dependent on your operating system.

These commands will check for their presence:

```
$ cc --version
i686-apple-darwin10-gcc-4.2.1 (GCC) 4.2.1 (Apple Inc. build 5666) (dot 3)
Copyright (C) 2007 Free Software Foundation, Inc.
This is free software; see the source for copying conditions.  There is
NO
warranty; not even for MERCHANTABILITY or FITNESS FOR A PARTICULAR
PURPOSE.
$ python
Python 2.6.6 (r266:84292, Feb 15 2011, 01:35:25)
[GCC 4.2.1 (Apple Inc. build 5664)] on darwin
Type "help", "copyright", "credits" or "license" for more information.
>>>
```

Installing developer tools on Mac OS X

The developer tools (such as GCC) are an optional installation on Mac OS X. There are two ways to get those tools, both of which are free. On the OS X, installing DVD is a directory labeled "Optional Installs", in which there is a package installer for—among other things—the developer tools, including Xcode:

The other method is to download the latest copy of Xcode (for free) from: http://developer.apple.com/xcode/

Installing in your home directory

It used to be preferred for developers to install Node in their home directory for developing applications. Recent changes with Node 0.4.x and more, especially npm 1.0, have made it less necessary to do so. You may prefer to install Node in a system-wide directory, which we cover in the next section, or you may prefer to have local Node installs for testing or development.

Let's see how to do a local Node install:

1. First, download the source from http://nodejs.org/#download. One way to do this is with your browser, and another way is as follows:

    ```
    $ mkdir src
    $ cd src
    $ wget http://nodejs.org/dist/node-v0.4.8.tar.gz
    $ tar xvfz node-v0.4.8.tar.gz
    $ cd node-v0.4.8
    ```

2. The next step is to configure the source so that it can be built. It includes the typical sort of configure script and you can see its long list of options by running ./configure -help. To cause the installation to land in your home directory run it this way:

    ```
    $ ./configure --prefix=$HOME/node/0.4.8
    Checking for program g++ or c++        : /usr/bin/g++
    Checking for program cpp               : /usr/bin/cpp
    Checking for program ar                : /usr/bin/ar
    Checking for program ranlib            : /usr/bin/ranlib
    ...
    ```

    After a moment it'll stop and more likely successfully configure the source tree for installation in your chosen directory. If this doesn't succeed it will print a message about something that needs to be fixed. Once the configure script is satisfied you can go on to the next step.

3. With the configure script satisfied, you compile the software:

```
$ make
.. a long log of compiler output is printed
$ make install
```

4. Once installed you should make sure to add the installation directory to your PATH variable as follows:

```
$ echo 'export PATH=$HOME/node/0.4.8/bin:${PATH}' >>~/.bashrc
$ . ~/.bashrc
```

Or for csh users:

```
$ echo 'setenv PATH $HOME/node/0.4.8/bin:${PATH}' >>~/.cshrc
$ source ~/.cshrc
```

This should result in some directories like this:

```
$ ls ~/node/0.4.8/
bin     include      lib      share
$ ls ~/node/0.4.8/bin
node         node-waf
```

Once this is done you can skip ahead to the *Run a few commands; test your installation* section.

What's the rationale for a home directory installation?

There are two reasons to consider installing Node in your home directory:

- Testing and development
- Security considerations

First, developers may want to experiment with customized Node instances, test their application against several Node versions, or even hack on Node itself. In these (and other) cases, a home directory installation is preferred.

The security considerations issue may not be so obvious, so let's walk through it.

One version of this is those times when you're using a Unix-like system, have no administrator privileges, and want to use Node. A home directory Node install is easy to set up.

Another sort of security consideration is the downloading and executing of scripts while installing Node, or its associated tools (such as the Node Package Manager, npm). Can you trust the author of those tools? Maybe a 0.1.x or 0.2.x version number didn't carry with it a sense of stability or security. Whatever the reason, older versions of npm made scary noises whenever used under sudo, and a fairly rational reason was given.

Before npm 1.0, all modules had to be installed inside the Node instance. This might seem innocuous except for cases where Node is installed in a system-wide directory; this requires root privileges, and there are certain scripts that often run during package installation for package setup. You might not have root privileges, or your local security policies might prohibit willy-nilly downloading software to run as root. By installing Node in your home directory, any damage which might occur is limited to your home directory. Lucky you.

With Node 0.4.x and npm 1.0.x, the normal practice is now to install packages local to your application, rather than installing them within the Node instance. This can be done without requiring root privileges.

Because of this it is possible today to have an administrator controlled Node instance in a system-wide directory, and still install any desired package local to your application because of a flexible package discovery algorithm. We'll go over this in depth in the next chapter.

Installing in a system-wide directory

For normal use, you would install Node in a system-wide directory. Some reasons are:

- It's a normal everyday best practice
- It enables sharing the Node install between different applications or people
- It prevents inadvertently overwriting files in the Node install
- It allows you to launch Node servers at system boot time

Installing in a system-wide directory is almost identical to a home directory installation, with just two differences:

- The first difference is selecting the installation directory. We do this with the configure script, and by default (with no-prefix= option) it will install in /usr/local:

```
$ ./configure          # for /usr/local
$ ./configure -prefix=/usr/local/node/0.4.8
```

Basically, choose your directory and use `configure` to do it.

- The second difference is the `make install` step. Since system-wide directories are almost always protected against regular users writing files in them, you will need to do the install with root privileges as follows:

```
$ sudo make install
```

You should note that if you install Node in a directory already in your PATH variable, you won't need to change it.

Installing on Mac OS X with MacPorts

You can of course install Node on Mac OS X using the previously described methods. They work perfectly thanks to it being a UNIX compatible system.

The MacPorts project (http://www.macports.org/) has for years been packaging a long list of open source software packages for Mac OS X, and they have packaged Node. After you have installed MacPorts using the installer on their website, installing Node is pretty much this simple:

```
$ sudo port search nodejs
nodejs @0.4.8 (devel, net)
    Evented I/O for V8 JavaScript
$ sudo port install nodejs
.. long log of downloading and installing prerequisites and Node
```

However, npm is not available to be installed this way.

Installing on Mac OS X with homebrew

Homebrew is another open source software package manager for Mac OS X, which some say is the perfect replacement for MacPorts. It is available through their home page at http://mxcl.github.com/homebrew/. After installing homebrew using the instructions on their website, using it to install Node is as simple as this:

```
$ brew search node
leafnode   node
$ brew install node
==> Downloading http://nodejs.org/dist/node-v0.4.8.tar.gz
################################################### 100.0%
==> ./configure --prefix=/usr/local/Cellar/node/0.4.8
==> make install
```

```
.. etc
$ brew search npm
npm can be installed thusly by following the instructions at
  http://npmjs.org/
```

Installing on Linux from package management systems

While it's still premature for Linux distros or other operating systems to pre-package Node with their OS, that doesn't mean you cannot install it using the package managers. Instructions on the Node wiki currently list packaged versions of Node for Debian, Ubuntu, OpenSUSE, and Arch Linux.

See: `https://github.com/joyent/node/wiki/Installing-Node.js-via-package-manager`

For example on Debian:

```
# echo deb http://ftp.us.debian.org/debian/ sid main > /etc/apt/sources.
list.d/sid.list
# apt-get update
# apt-get install nodejs # Documentation is great.
```

And on Ubuntu:

```
# sudo apt-get install python-software-properties
# sudo add-apt-repository ppa:jerome-etienne/neoip
# sudo apt-get update
# sudo apt-get install nodejs
```

We can expect in due course that the Linux distros and other operating systems will be routinely bundling Node into the OS like they do with other languages today.

Maintaining multiple Node installs simultaneously

Normally you won't have multiple versions of Node installed and doing so adds complexity to your system. But if you are hacking on Node itself, or are testing against different Node releases, or any of several similar situations, you may want to have multiple Node installations. The method to do so is a simple variation on what we've already discussed.

If you noticed during the instructions discussed earlier, the `-prefix` option was used in a way that directly supports installing several Node versions side-by-side in the same directory:

```
$ ./configure --prefix=$HOME/node/0.4.8
```

And:

```
$ ./configure --prefix=/usr/local/node/0.4.8
```

This initial step determines the install directory. Clearly when version 0.4.9 or version 0.6.1 or whichever version is released, you can change the install prefix to have the new version installed side-by-side with previous versions.

To switch between Node versions is simply a matter of changing the PATH variable (on POSIX systems), as follows:

```
$ export PATH=/usr/local/node/0.6.1/bin:${PATH}
```

It starts to be a little tedious to maintain this after a while. For each release, you have to set up Node, npm, and any third-party modules you desire in your Node install; also the command shown to change your PATH is not quite optimal. Inventive programmers have created several version managers to make this easier by automatically setting up not only Node, but npm also, and providing commands to change your PATH the smart way:

- `https://github.com/visionmedia/n` – Node version manager
- `https://github.com/kuno/neco` – Nodejs Ecosystem COordinator

Run a few commands; test your installation

Now that you've installed Node we want to do two things, verify that the installation was successful, and familiarize you with the command-line tools.

Node's command-line tools

The basic install of Node includes two commands, `node` and `node-waf`. We've already seen `node` in action. It's used either for running command-line scripts, or server processes. The other, `node-waf`, is a build tool for Node native extensions. Since it's for building native extensions we will not cover it in this book and you should consult the online documentation at `nodejs.org`.

The easiest way to verify your Node installation works is also the best way to get help with Node. Type the following:

```
$ node --help
Usage: node [options] script.js [arguments]
Options:
  -v, --version          print node's version
  --debug[=port]         enable remote debugging via given TCP port
                         without stopping the execution
  --debug-brk[=port]     as above, but break in script.js and
                         wait for remote debugger to connect
  --v8-options           print v8 command line options
  --vars                 print various compiled-in variables
  --max-stack-size=val set max v8 stack size (bytes)


Enviromental variables:
NODE_PATH                ':'-separated list of directories
                         prefixed to the module search path,
                         require.paths.
NODE_DEBUG               Print additional debugging output.
NODE_MODULE_CONTEXTS     Set to 1 to load modules in their own
                         global contexts.
NODE_DISABLE_COLORS  Set to 1 to disable colors in the REPL
Documentation can be found at http://nodejs.org/ or with 'man node'
```

It prints the USAGE message giving you the command-line options.

Notice that there are options for both Node and V8 (not shown in the previous command line). Remember that Node is built on top of V8; it has its own universe of options that largely focus on details of bytecode compilation or the garbage collection and heap algorithms. Enter node --v8-options to see the full list of them.

On the command line you can specify options, a single script file, and a list of arguments to that script. We'll discuss script arguments further in the next section.

Running Node with no arguments plops you in an interactive JavaScript shell:

```
$ node
> console.log('Hello, world!');
Hello, world!
> console.log(JSON.stringify(require.paths));
["/Users/davidherron/.node_libraries","/opt/local/lib/node"]
```

Any code you can write in a Node script can be written here. The command interpreter gives a good terminal-orientated user experience and is useful for interactively playing with your code. You do play with your code, don't you? Good!

Running a simple script with Node

Now let's see how to run scripts with Node. It's quite simple and let's start by referring back to the help message:

```
$ node --help
Usage: node [options] script.js [arguments]
```

It's just a script filename and some script arguments, which should be familiar for anyone who has written scripts in other languages.

First create a text file named ls.js with the following content:

```
var fs = require('fs');
var files = fs.readdirSync('.');
for (fn in files) {
  console.log(files[fn]);
}
```

> **Downloading the example code**
>
> You can download the example code files for all Packt books you have purchased from your account at http://www.PacktPub.com. If you purchased this book elsewhere, you can visit http://www.PacktPub.com/support and register to have the files e-mailed directly to you.

Next run it by typing the command:

```
$ node ls.js
app.js
ls.js
```

This is a pale cheap imitation of the Unix ls command (as if you couldn't figure that out from the name). The readdirSync function is a close analogue to the Unix readdir system call (type man 3 readdir to learn more) and is used to list the files in a directory.

The script arguments land in a global array named process.argv and you can modify ls.js as follows to see how this array works:

```
var fs = require('fs');
var dir = '.';
if (process.argv[2]) dir = process.argv[2];
var files = fs.readdirSync(dir);
```

```
for (fn in files) {
  console.log(files[fn]);
}
```

And you can run it as follows:

```
$ node ls2.js ../0.4.8/bin
node
node-waf
```

Launching a server with Node

Many scripts that you'll run are server processes. We'll be running lots of these scripts later on. Since we're still in the dual mode of verifying the installation and familiarizing you with using Node, we want to run a simple HTTP server. Let's borrow the simple server script on the Node home page (`http://nodejs.org`).

Create a file named `app.js` containing:

```
var http = require('http');
http.createServer(function (req, res) {
  res.writeHead(200, {'Content-Type': 'text/plain'});
  res.end('Hello, World!\n');
}).listen(8124, '127.0.0.1');
console.log('Server running at http://127.0.0.1:8124');
```

And run it this way:

```
$ node app.js
Server running at http://127.0.0.1:8124
```

This is the simplest of web servers you can build with Node. If you're interested in how it works flip forward to Chapters 4-6. At the moment just visit `http://127.0.0.1:8124` in your browser to see the following:

A question to ponder is why did this script not exit, when `ls.js` did exit. In both cases execution of the script reaches the end of the script; in `app.js` the Node process does not exist, while in `ls.js` it does. The reason is the presence of active event listeners. Node always starts up an event loop, and in `app.js` the `.listen` function creates an event `listener` which implements the HTTP protocol. This event listener keeps `app.js` running until you do something like type `Control-C` in the terminal window. In `ls.js` there is nothing which creates a long-running event listener, so when `ls.js` reaches the end of its script Node will exit.

Installing npm—the Node package manager

Node by itself is a pretty basic system, being a JavaScript interpreter with a few interesting asynchronous I/O libraries. One of the things which makes Node interesting is the rapidly growing ecosystem of third party modules for Node. At the center of that ecosystem is npm. The modules can be downloaded as source and assembled manually for use with Node programs. npm gives us a simpler way; npm is the de-facto standard package manager for Node and it greatly simplifies downloading and using these modules. We will talk about npm at length in the next chapter.

To install npm, type this command shown on the `npmjs.org` home page:

```
$ curl http://npmjs.org/install.sh | sh
```

This downloads and executes a shell script on your system, and maybe you should consider first typing this command to see if you're comfortable with the shell script:

```
$ curl http://npmjs.org/install.sh | less
```

This installs the npm script and package inside a Node installation tree. This means you need to take some care in two situations to do this correctly.

If you've had to set the PATH variable to run Node, then make sure PATH is set correctly when running the npm installer as follows:

```
$ export PATH=/path/to/node/0.n.y/bin:${PATH}
$ curl http://npmjs.org/install.sh | sh
```

The next consideration is if Node is installed in a system-wide directory which required installation with `sudo make install`. If so, the installation should be done this way:

```
$ curl http://npmjs.org/install.sh | sudo sh
```

Using `sudo sh` means the process that's doing the work to install npm (`/bin/sh`) is run with root privileges under `sudo`.

Now that we have npm installed let's take it for a quick spin:

```
$ npm install -g hexy
/home/david/node/0.4.7/bin/hexy -> /home/david/node/0.4.7/lib/node_
modules/hexy/bin/hexy_cmd.js
hexy@0.2.1 /home/david/node/0.4.7/lib/node_modules/hexy
$ hexy --width 12 ls.js
00000000: 7661 7220 6673 203d 2072 6571  var.fs.=.req
0000000c: 7569 7265 2827 6673 2729 3b0a  uire('fs');.
00000018: 7661 7220 6669 6c65 7320 3d20  var.files.=.
00000024: 6673 2e72 6561 6464 6972 5379  fs.readdirSy
00000030: 6e63 2827 2e27 293b 0a66 6f72  nc('.');.for
0000003c: 2028 666e 2069 6e20 6669 6c65  .(fn.in.file
00000048: 7329 207b 0a20 2063 6f6e 736f  s).{...conso
00000054: 6c65 2e6c 6f67 2866 696c 6573  le.log(files
00000060: 5b66 6e5d 293b 0a7d 0a        [fn]);.}.
```

Again, we'll be doing a deep dive into npm in the next chapter. The `hexy` utility is both a Node library and a script for printing out these old style hex dumps.

Starting Node servers at system startup

Earlier we started a Node server from the command line. While this is useful for testing and development, it's not useful for deploying an application in any normal sense. There are normal practices for starting server processes, which differ for each operating system. Implementing a Node server means starting it similarly to the other background processes (sshd, apache, mysql, and so on) using, for example, start/stop scripts.

The Node project does not include start/stop scripts for any operating system. It can be argued that it would be out of place for Node to include such scripts. Instead, Node server applications should include such scripts. The traditional way is that the `init` daemon manages background processes using scripts in the `/etc/init.d` directory. On Fedora and Redhat that's still the process, but other operating systems use other daemon managers such as Upstart or launchd.

Writing these start/stop scripts is only part of what's required. Web servers have to be reliable (for example auto-restarting on crashes), manageable (integrate well with system management practices), observable (saving STDOUT to logfiles), and so on. Node is more like a construction kit with the pieces and parts for building servers, and is not a complete polished server itself. Implementing a complete web server based on Node means scripting to integrate with the background process management on your OS, implementing the logging features you need, the security practices or defenses against bad behavior such as denial of service attacks, and much more.

Here are several tools or methods for integrating Node servers with background process management on several operating systems, to implement continuous server presence beginning at system start-up. In a moment we'll also do a brief walkthrough of using Forever on a Debian server. The following is a list of ways to run Node as a background daemon on different platforms:

- nodejs-autorestart (`https://github.com/shimondoodkin/nodejs-autorestart`) manages a Node instance on Linux which uses Upstart (Ubuntu, Debian, and so on).

- fugue (`https://github.com/pgte/fugue`) watches a Node server, restarting it if it crashes.

- forever (`https://github.com/indexzero/forever`) is a small command-line Node script which ensures a script will run "forever". For a definition of "forever", Charlie Robbins wrote a blog post (`http://blog.nodejitsu.com/keep-a-nodejs-server-up-with-forever`) about its use.

- node-init (`https://github.com/frodwith/node-init`) is a Node script which turns your Node application into a LSB-compliant init script. LSB being a specification of Linux compatibility.

- Debian's `launchtool` (`http://people.debian.org/~enrico/launchtool.html`) is a system command for supervising the launch of any command, including running it as a daemon.

- Ubuntu's Upstart tool (`http://upstart.ubuntu.com/`) can be used alone (`http://caolanmcmahon.com/posts/deploying_node_js_with_upstart`) or along with `monit` (`http://howtonode.org/deploying-node-upstart-monit`) to manage a Node server.

- On Mac OS X one writes a `launchd` script. Apple has published a guide on implementing `launchd` scripts at `http://developer.apple.com/library/mac/documentation/MacOSX/Conceptual/BPSystemStartup/Articles/LaunchOnDemandDaemons.html`.

To demonstrate a little bit of what's involved let's use the forever tool, along with an LSB-style init script, to implement a little Node server process. The server is a Debian based VPS with Node and npm installed in /usr/local/node/0.4.8. The following server script is in /usr/local/app.js (not the most correct place to install the app, but useful for this demo):

```
#!/usr/bin/env node
var http = require('http');
http.createServer(function (req, res) {
  res.writeHead(200, {'Content-Type': 'text/plain'});
  res.end('Hello World\n');
}).listen(1337);
```

Note the first line of the script carefully. It is a little bit of Unix/POSIX magic that helps to make the script executable.

The forever tool is installed as follows:

```
$ sudo npm install -g forever
```

Forever manages background processes. It can restart them on crashes, send the standard output and error streams to log files, and has several other useful features. It's worth exploring.

The final bit is a script, /etc/init.d/node, modified from another /etc/init.d script:

```
#! /bin/sh -e
set -e
PATH=/usr/local/node/0.4.8/bin:/bin:/usr/bin:/sbin:/usr/sbin
DAEMON=/usr/local/app.js
case "$1" in
  start) forever start $DAEMON ;;
  stop)  forever stop  $DAEMON ;;
  force-reload|restart)
    forever restart $DAEMON ;;
  *) echo "Usage: /etc/init.d/node {start|stop|restart|force-reload}"
    exit 1
    ;;
esac
exit 0
```

On Debian you set up an init script with this command:

```
$ sudo /usr/sbin/update-rc.d node defaults
```

This configures your system so that /etc/init.d/node is invoked on reboot and shutdown to start or stop the background process. During boot-up or shutdown each init script is executed, and its first argument is either start or stop. Therefore, when our init script is executed during boot-up or shutdown one of these two lines will be executed:

```
start) forever start $DAEMON ;;
stop)  forever stop  $DAEMON ;;
```

We can run the init script manually:

```
$ sudo /etc/init.d/node start
info: Running action: start
info: Forever processing file: /usr/local/app.js
```

Because our init script uses the forever tool, we can ask forever the status of all processes it has started:

```
$ sudo forever list
info: Running action: list
info: Forever processes running
    [0] node /usr/local/app.js [16666, 16664] /home/me/.forever/7rd6.log
0:0:1:24.817
```

With the server process running on your server you can open it in a browser window:

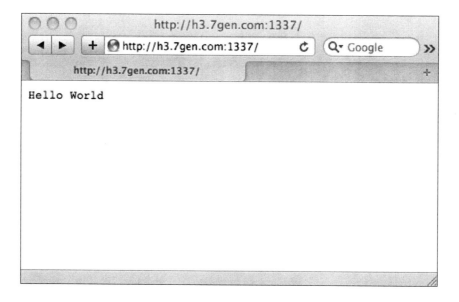

With the server still running and managed by forever we have these processes:

```
$ ps ax | grep node
16664 ? Ssl 0:00 node /usr/local/node/0.4.8/bin/forever start /usr/local/
app.js
16666 ? S    0:00 node /usr/local/app.js
```

When you're done playing with this you can shut it down this way:

```
$ sudo /etc/init.d/node stop
info: Running action: stop
info: Forever processing file: /usr/local/app.js
info: Forever stopped process:
   [0] node /usr/local/app.js [5712, 5711] /home/me/.forever/Gtex.log
0:0:0:28.777
$ sudo forever list
info: Running action: list
info: No forever processes running
```

Using all CPU cores on multi-core systems

V8 is a single thread JavaScript engine. This is good enough for the Chrome browser but it means a Node based server on that shiny new 16 core server will have one CPU core going flat out, and 15 CPU cores sitting idle. Your manager may want an explanation for this.

A single thread process will only use one core. That's a fact of life. Using multiple cores in a single process requires multi-threaded software. But Node's *no threads design paradigm*, while keeping the programming model simple, also means that Node does not make use of multiple cores. What are you to do? Or more importantly, how are you to keep your manager happy?

Several projects are working on multi-process Node configurations for greater reliability and to also use all the cores in multi-core server hardware.

The basic idea is to start multiple Node processes, sharing request traffic between them. With a cluster of single thread processes you can use all the cores, and keep your manager happy about the server investment.

One of the multi-process Node server projects, Cluster (`https://github.com/LearnBoost/cluster`), is an "extensible multi-core server manager for Node.js". It starts up a configurable set of child processes, restarting them if they crash, and has extensive logging, command-line control utilities, and statistics. The older Spark project has closed itself in favor of the Cluster project.

The Cluster project includes a few example server configurations that shows what it can do. Let's install it and use one of the examples to see how it works:

```
$ sudo npm install cluster
cluster@0.6.4 ./node_modules/cluster
└── log@1.2.0
```

Using one of the examples (`reload.js`) as a model, we'll modify `app.js` to create `cluster-app.js` containing the following:

```
#!/usr/bin/env node
var http = require('http');
var cluster = require('cluster');
var server = http.createServer(function (req, res) {
  res.writeHead(200, {'Content-Type': 'text/plain'});
  res.end('Hello World\n');
})
cluster(server).set('workers', 2).use(cluster.reload())
  .listen(1337);
```

This cluster configuration creates two worker processes for sharing the load, and will automatically reload modified files. You can read the documentation on the Cluster project site for more details.

It can be run as `node cluster-app.js`, but let's modify `/etc/init.d/node` to run it instead. It's done simply by setting the DAEMON variable to this value:

```
DAEMON=/usr/local/cluster-app.js
```

Then:

```
$ sudo /etc/init.d/node start
info: Running action: start
info: Forever processing file: /usr/local/cluster-app.js
$ sudo forever list
info: Running action: list
info: Forever processes running
  [0] node /usr/local/cluster-app.js [6522, 6521]
$ ps ax | grep node
```

```
  6521 ? Ssl 0:00 node /usr/local/node/0.4.8/bin/forever start /usr/local/
cluster-app.js
  6522 ? Sl  0:15 node /usr/local/cluster-app.js
  6541 ? S   0:00 /usr/local/node/0.4.8/bin/node  /usr/local/cluster-app.
js
  6542 ? S   0:00 /usr/local/node/0.4.8/bin/node /usr/local/cluster-app.js
```

Now you have a multi-process Node server running. We see the two processes with
ps, and you can verify it's running by visiting the http://example.com:1337/ URL
in your browser to see the "**Hello, World**" message. But because it's using Cluster's
auto-reload feature you can then make a suitable modification to cluster-app.js:
click reload in the browser (no need to restart the server) and you will see something
like this:

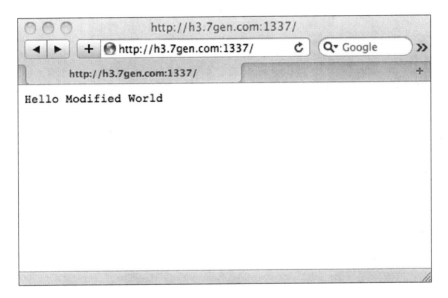

Summary

We learned a lot in this chapter, about installing Node, using its command-line tools, and how to run a Node server. We also breezed past a lot of details that will be covered later in the book, so be patient.

Specifically, we covered:

- Downloading and compiling the Node source code
- Installing Node either for development use in your home directory, or for deployment in system directories
- Installing npm, the de-facto standard Node Package Manager
- Running Node scripts or Node servers
- What's required to use Node for a reliable background process
- Using multiple processes to use all CPU cores

Now that we've seen how to set up the basic system, we're ready to start working on implementing applications with Node. First we must learn the basic building block of Node applications, modules, which is the topic of the next chapter.

3
Node Modules

Before writing Node applications we must learn about Node modules and packages. Modules and packages are the building blocks for breaking down your application into smaller pieces.

In this chapter we shall:

- Learn what a module is
- Learn about the CommonJS module specification
- Learn how Node finds modules
- Learn about the npm package management system

So let's get on with it.

What's a module?

Modules are the basic building block of constructing Node applications. We have already seen modules in action; every JavaScript file we use in Node is itself a module. It's time to see what they are and how they work.

In the `ls.js` example in *Chapter 2*, *Setting up Node*, we wrote the following code to pull in the `fs` module, giving us access to its functions:

```
var fs = require('fs');
```

The `require` function searches for modules, and loads the module definition into the Node runtime, making its functions available. The `fs` object (in this case) contains the code (and data) exported by the `fs` module.

Let's look at a brief example of this before we start diving into the details. Ponder over this module, `simple.js`:

```
var count = 0;
exports.next = function() { return count++; }
```

This defines an exported function and a local variable. Now let's use it:

```
$ node
> var s = require('./simple');
> s.next();
0
> s.next();
1
> s.next();
2
> s.next();
3
> $
```

The object returned from `require('./simple')` is the same object, `exports`, we assigned a function to inside `simple.js`. Each call to `s.next` calls the function `next` in `simple.js`, which returns (and increments) the value of the `count` variable, explaining why `s.next` returns progressively bigger numbers.

The rule is that, anything (functions, objects) assigned as a field of `exports` is exported from the module, and objects inside the module but not assigned to `exports` are not visible to any code outside the module. This is an example of encapsulation.

Now that we've got a taste of modules, let's take a deeper look.

Node modules

Node's module implementation is strongly inspired by, but not identical to, the CommonJS module specification (described at the end of this chapter). The differences between them might only be important if you need to share code between Node and other CommonJS systems. A quick scan of the Modules/1.1.1 spec indicates that the differences are minor, and for our purposes it's enough to just get on with the task of learning to use Node without dwelling too long on the differences.

How does Node resolve require('module')?

In Node, modules are stored in files, one module per file. There are several ways to specify module names, and several ways to organize the deployment of modules in the file system. It's quite flexible, especially when used with npm, the de-facto standard package manager for Node.

Module identifiers and path names

Generally speaking the module name is a path name, but with the file extension removed. That is, when we wrote `require('./simple')` earlier, Node knew to add `.js` to the file name and load in `simple.js`.

Modules whose file names end in `.js` are of course expected to be written in JavaScript. Node also supports binary code native libraries as Node modules. In this case the file name extension to use is `.node`. It's outside our scope to discuss implementation of a native code Node module, but this gives you enough knowledge to recognize them when you come across them.

Some Node modules are not files in the file system, but are baked into the Node executable. These are the Core modules, the ones documented on `nodejs.org`. Their original existence is as files in the Node source tree but the build process compiles them into the binary Node executable.

There are three types of module identifiers: relative, absolute, and top-level.

Relative module identifiers begin with "`./`" or "`../`" and absolute identifiers begin with "`/`". These are identical with POSIX file system semantics with path names being relative to the file being executed.

Absolute module identifiers obviously are relative to the root of the file system.

Top-level module identifiers do not begin with "`.`" , "`..`", or "`/`" and instead are simply the module name. These modules are stored in one of several directories, such as a `node_modules` directory, or those directories listed in the array `require.paths`, designated by Node to hold these modules. These are discussed later.

Local modules within your application

The universe of all possible modules is split neatly into two kinds, those modules that are part of a specific application, and those modules that aren't. Hopefully the modules that aren't part of a specific application were written to serve a generalized purpose. Let's begin with implementation of modules used within your application.

Typically your application will have a directory structure of module files sitting next to each other in the source control system, and then deployed to servers. These modules will know the relative path to their sibling modules within the application, and should use that knowledge to refer to each other using relative module identifiers.

For example, to help us understand this, let's look at the structure of an existing Node package, the Express web application framework. It includes several modules structured in a hierarchy that the Express developers found to be useful. You can imagine creating a similar hierarchy for applications reaching a certain level of complexity, subdividing the application into chunks larger than a module but smaller than an application. Unfortunately there isn't a word to describe this, in Node, so we're left with a clumsy phrase like "*subdivide into chunks larger than a module*". Each subdivided chunk would be implemented as a directory with a few modules in it.

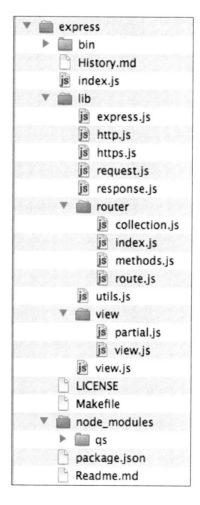

In this example, the most likely relative module reference is to `utils.js`. Depending on the source file which wants to use `utils.js` it would use one of the following `require` statements:

```
var utils = require('./lib/utils');
var utils = require('./utils');
var utils = require('../utils');
```

Bundling external dependencies with your application

Modules placed in a `node_modules` directory are required using a top-level module identifier such as:

```
var express = require('express');
```

Node searches the `node_modules` directories to find modules. There is not just one `node_modules` directory, but several that are searched for by Node. Node starts at the directory of the current module, appends `node_modules`, and searches there for the module being requested. If not found in that `node_modules` directory it moves to the parent directory and tries again, repeatedly moving to parent directories until reaching the root of the file system.

In the previous example, you'll notice a `node_modules` directory within which is a directory named qs. By being situated in that location, the qs module is available to any module inside Express with this code utterance:

```
var qs = require('qs');
```

What if you want to use the Express framework in your application? That's simple, make a `node_modules` directory inside the directory structure of your application, and install the Express framework there:

We can see this in a hypothetical application shown here, `drawapp`. With the `node_modules` directory situated where it is any module within `drawapp` can access `express` with the code:

```
var express = require('express');
```

But those same modules cannot access the `qs` module stashed inside the `node_modules` directory within the `express` module. The search for `node_modules` directories containing the desired module goes upward in the filesystem hierarchy, and not into child directories.

Likewise a module could be installed in `lib/node_modules` and be accessible from `draw.js` or `svg.js` and not accessible from `index.js`. The search for `node_modules` directories goes upward, and not into child directories.

Node searches upward for `node_modules` directories, stopping at the first place it finds the module it's searching for. A module reference from `draw.js` or `svg.js` would search this list of directories:

- `/home/david/projects/drawapp/lib/node_modules`
- `/home/david/projects/drawapp/node_modules`
- `/home/david/projects/node_modules`
- `/home/david/node_modules`
- `/home/node_modules`
- `/node_modules`

The `node_modules` directory plays a key role in keeping the Node package management from disappearing into a maze of conflicting package versions. Rather than having one place to put modules, and descend into confusion as dependencies on conflicting module versions slowly drive you nuts, multiple `node_modules` directories let you have specific versions of modules in specific places, if needed. Different versions of the same module can live in different `node_modules` directories, and they won't conflict with each other, so long as the `node_modules` directories are situated correctly.

For example, if you've written an application using the `forms` module (`https://github.com/caolan/forms`) to help build the forms in your application and after writing hundreds of different forms, the authors of the `forms` module make incompatible changes. With hundreds of forms to convert and test on their new API you might not want to do it all at once, but spread out the effort. To do so would require two directories within your application, each with its own `node_modules` directory, with a different version of the `forms` module in each. Then as you convert a form to the new `forms` module, move its code into the directory where the new `forms` module lives.

System-wide modules in the require.paths directories

The algorithm Node uses to find the `node_modules` directories extends beyond your application source tree. It goes to the root of the file system, and you could have a `/node_modules` directory with a global module repository to satisfy any search for modules.

Node provides an additional mechanism with the `require.paths` variable. This is an array of directory names where we can search for modules.

An example is:

```
$ node
> require.paths;
["/home/david/.node_modules","/home/david/.node_libraries","/usr/local/
lib/node"]
```

The NODE_PATH environment variable can add directories to the require.paths array:

```
$ export NODE_PATH=/usr/lib/node
$ node
> require.paths;
["/usr/lib/node","/home/david/.node_libraries","/usr/local/lib/node"]
>
```

It used to be a common idiom for Node programs to add directories into require. paths variable as follows: require.paths.push(__dirname). However, this is no longer recommended because in practice it was found to be a troublesome source of confusion. While you can still do this, and while there are still modules in existence using this idiom, it's sternly frowned upon. The results are unpredictable when multiple modules push directories into require.paths.

The recommended practice is, in most cases, to install modules in node_modules directories.

Complex modules—modules as directories

A complex module might include several internal modules, data files, template files, documentation, tests, or more. These can be stashed inside a carefully constructed directory structure,which Node will treat as a module satisfying a require('moduleName') request. To do so, you place one of the two files in a directory, either a module file named index.js, or a file named package.json. The package.json file will contain data describing the module, in a format nearly identical to the package.json format defined by the npm package manager (described later). The two are compatible with Node using a very small subset of the tags that npm recognizes.

Specifically, Node recognizes these fields in package.json:

```
{ name: "myAwesomeLibrary",
  main: "./lib/awesome.js" }
```

With that `package.json`, the code `require('myAwesomeLibrary')` would find this directory, and load the file:

```
/path/to/node_modules/myAwesomeLibrary/lib/awesome.js
```
If there were no `package.json` file then Node will instead look for `index.js`, which would load the file:

```
/path/to/node_modules/myAwesomeLibrary/index.js
```

Under either scenario (`index.js` or `package.json`), the complex module with internal modules and other assets is easy to implement. Referring back to the Express package structure we looked at earlier, some of the modules will use relative module identifiers to reference other modules inside the package, and you can use a `node_modules` directory to integrate modules developed elsewhere.

Node package Manager (npm)

As described in *Chapter 2, Setting up Node*, npm is a package management and distribution system for Node. It has become the de-facto standard for distributing modules (packages) for use with Node. Conceptually it's similar to tools like apt-get (Debian), rpm/yum (Redhat/Fedora), MacPorts (Mac OS X), CPAN (Perl), or PEAR (PHP). It's purpose is publishing and distributing Node packages over the Internet using a simple command-line interface. With npm you can quickly find packages to serve specific purposes, download them, install them, and manage packages you've already installed.

npm defines a package format for Node largely based on the CommonJS Package spec.

npm package format

An npm package is a directory structure with a `package.json` file describing the package. This is exactly what we just referred to as a Complex Module, except npm recognizes many more `package.json` tags than does Node. The starting point for npm's `package.json` is the CommonJS Packages/1.0 specification. The documentation for npm's `package.json` implementation is accessed with the following command:

```
$ npm help json
```

A basic `package.json` file is as follows:

```
{ name: "packageName",
  version: "1.0",
  main: "mainModuleName",
```

```
    modules: {
      "mod1": "lib/mod1",
      "mod2": "lib/mod2"
    }
  }
```

The file is in JSON format which, as a JavaScript programmer, you should already have seen a few hundred times.

The most important tags are `name` and `version`. The name will appear in URLs and command names, so choose one that's safe for both. If you desire to publish a package in the public npm repository it's helpful to check and see if a particular name is already being used, at `http://search.npmjs.org` or with the following command:

```
$ npm search packageName
```

The `main` tag is treated the same as we discussed in the previous section on complex modules. It references the module that will be returned when invoking `require('packageName')`. Packages can contain many modules within themselves, and those can be listed in the `modules` list.

Packages can be bundled as tar-gzip tarballs, especially to send them over the Internet.

A package can declare dependencies on other packages. That way npm can automatically install other modules required by the module being installed. Dependencies are declared as follows:

```
    "dependencies":
      { "foo" : "1.0.0 - 2.9999.9999"
      , "bar" : ">=1.0.2 <2.1.2"
      }
```

The description and keywords fields help people to find the package when searching in an npm repository (`http://search.npmjs.org`). Ownership of a package can be documented in the homepage, author, or contributors fields:

```
    "description": "My wonderful packages walks dogs",
      "homepage": "http://npm.dogs.org/dogwalker/",
      "author": dogwhisperer@dogs.org
```

Some npm packages provide executable programs meant to be in the user's PATH. These are declared using the `bin` tag. It's a map of command names to the script which implements that command. The command scripts are installed into the directory containing the node executable using the name given.

```
bin: {
  'nodeload.js': './nodeload.js',
    'nl.js': './nl.js'
},
```

The `directories` tag documents the package directory structure. The `lib` directory is automatically scanned for modules to load. There are other directory tags for binaries, manuals, and documentation.

```
directories: { lib: './lib', bin: './bin' },
```

The script tags are script commands run at various events in the lifecycle of the package. These events include `install`, `activate`, `uninstall`, `update`, and more. For more information about script commands, use the following command:

```
$ npm help scripts
```

This was only a taste of the npm package format; see the documentation (`npm help json`) for more.

Finding npm packages

By default npm modules are retrieved over the Internet from the public package registry maintained on `http://npmjs.org`. If you know the module name it can be installed simply by typing the following:

```
$ npm install moduleName
```

But what if you don't know the module name? How do you discover the interesting modules?

The website `http://npmjs.org` publishes an index of the modules in that registry, and the `http://search.npmjs.org` site lets you search that index.

npm also has a command-line search function to consult the same index:

```
$ npm search mp3
mediatags  Tools extracting for media meta-data tags  =coolaj86  util m4a
aac mp3 id3 jpeg exiv xmp
node3p    An Amazon MP3 downloader for NodeJS.        =ncb000gt
```

Of course upon finding a module it's installed as follows:

```
$ npm install mediatags
```

After installing a module one may want to see the documentation, which would be on the module's website. The `homepage` tag in the `package.json` lists that URL. The easiest way to look at the `package.json` file is with the `npm view` command, as follows:

```
$ npm view zombie
...
{ name: 'zombie',
  description: 'Insanely fast, full-stack, headless browser testing using
Node.js',
...
  version: '0.9.4',
  homepage: 'http://zombie.labnotes.org/',
...
npm ok
```

You can use `npm view` to extract any tag from `package.json`, like the following which lets you view just the homepage tag:

```
$ npm view zombie homepage
http://zombie.labnotes.org/
```

Using the npm commands

The main npm command has a long list of sub-commands for specific package management operations. These cover every aspect of the lifecycle of publishing packages (as a package author), and downloading, using, or removing packages (as an npm consumer).

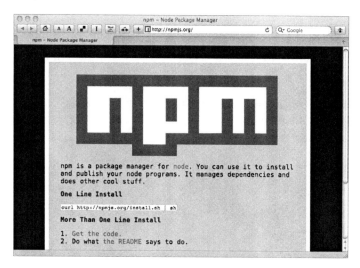

Getting help with npm

Perhaps the most important thing is to learn where to turn to get help. The main help is delivered along with the npm command accessed as follows:

```
Terminal — bash — 71×15

$ npm help

Usage: npm <command>

where <command> is one of:
    adduser, author, bin, c, cache, completion, config,
    deprecate, docs, edit, explore, faq, find, get, help, i,
    info, init, install, la, link, list, ll, ln, ls, outdated,
    owner, prefix, prune, publish, r, rb, rebuild, restart, rm,
    root, run-script, s, se, search, set, start, stop, tag,
    test, un, uninstall, unlink, unpublish, up, update, version,
    view, whoami

Add -h to any command for quick help.
```

For most of the commands you can access the help text for that command by typing the following:

```
$ npm help <command>
```

The npm website (http://npmjs.org/) has a FAQ that is also delivered with the npm software. Perhaps the most important question (and answer) is: **Why does npm hate me?** *npm is not capable of hatred. It loves everyone, even you.*

Viewing package information

The npm view command treats the package.json file as data, letting you query that data using a dot-notation for JSON tags such as viewing the package dependencies:

```
$ npm view google-openid dependencies
{ express: '>= 0.0.1',
  openid: '>= 0.1.1 <= 0.1.1' }
```

The package.json file can include the package repository URL. Therefore, if you just want to retrieve the package source, use the following:

```
$ npm view openid repository.url
git://github.com/havard/node-openid.git
$ git clone git://github.com/havard/node-openid.git
Cloning into node-openid...
```

```
remote: Counting objects: 253, done.
remote: Compressing objects: 100% (253/253), done.
remote: Total 253 (delta 148), reused 0 (delta 0)
Receiving objects: 100% (253/253), 63.29 KiB, done.
Resolving deltas: 100% (148/148), done.
```

What version of Node is required for a package?

```
$ npm view openid engines
node >= 0.4.1
```

Installing an npm package

The `npm install` command makes it easy to install packages upon finding the one of your dreams as follows:

```
$ npm install openid
openid@0.1.6 ./node_modules/openid
$ ls node_modules/
openid
```

Notice that the package is installed in a local `node_modules` directory. Packages can be installed in other locations either by changing the current directory, or by telling npm to make a global install.For example, the following will set up a directory, `/var/www`, where `/var/www/node_modules` stores modules to be shared among several websites:

```
$ cd /var/www
$ npm install openid
openid@0.1.6 ./node_modules/openid
```

npm makes a distinction between global mode and local mode. Normally it operates in local mode and installs packages into a local `node_modules` directory next to your application code. In global mode packages are installed globally, meaning that they're installed into the Node installation (directories in `require.paths`) rather than a local `node_modules` directory.

The first method to install packages in global mode is to use the `-g` flag as follows:

```
$ npm install -g openid
openid@0.1.6 /usr/local/node/0.4.7/lib/node_modules/openid
$ which node
/usr/local/node/0.4.7/bin/node
```

The installation directory in global mode is based on where Node is installed for you.

The second method for global mode installation is to change npm configuration settings. There are many configuration settings, which we'll discuss in some time, and the relevant one for now is as follows:

```
$ npm set global=true
$ npm get global
true
$ npm install openid
openid@0.1.6 /usr/local/node/0.4.7/lib/node_modules/openid
```

To learn about all the folders npm uses enter the following command:

```
$ npm help folders
```

Using installed packages

The point of installing a package is to enable a Node program to access the module like the following:

```
var openid = require('openid');
```

What npm does is to help you set up conditions for this to work smoothly.

Some packages include inner modules that could themselves be useful to other software. For example, the current version of this openid module we've been picking on includes a base64 encode/decode module that could be useful for other software:

```
var base64 = require('openid/lib/base64').base64;
```

This runs a risk the openid module could change its implementation of its base64 encode/decode function, breaking your application. Some packages structured themselves to provide a family of related sub-modules accessed this way, and provide some guarantee of a stable API for the exposed sub-modules.

What packages are currently installed?

The npm list command lists the installed packages, based on a search from the current directory. Remember that Node searches for modules starting at the current directory of the code being executed. Therefore, the installed packages are relatively based on your current directory, depending on the content of node_modules directories above the current directory.

For example, notice how the listed modules changes based on which directory you are in:

```
Terminal — bash — 87×27

$ pwd
/Users/davidherron/Node.JS/chap03
$ npm list
/Users/davidherron/Node.JS
├── async@0.1.9
├─┬ connect@1.4.2
│ └── qs@0.1.0
├── ejs@0.4.2
├─┬ express@2.3.11
│ └── qs@0.1.0
└── mime@1.2.2
$ cd ../chap06
$ npm list
/Users/davidherron/Node.JS/chap06
├── colors@0.5.0
├── ejs@0.4.2
├─┬ express@2.3.6
│ ├── connect@1.4.1
│ ├── mime@1.2.2
│ └── qs@0.1.0
├── mongodb@0.9.4
├── mongoose@1.3.3
├── mongoq@0.0.4
├── openid@0.1.6
└── sqlite3@2.0.12
$ 
```

By default the list is shown in a tree structure, that isn't terribly useful as data to other commands as shown in the previous screenshot. The `parseable` configuration setting can make the output usable as data as follows:

```
$ npm set parseable=true
$ npm list
/home/david/Node/chap06
/home/david/Node/chap06/node_modules/ejs
/home/david/Node/chap06/node_modules/express
/home/david/Node/chap06/node_modules/express/node_modules/connect
/home/david/Node/chap06/node_modules/express/node_modules/mime
/home/david/Node/chap06/node_modules/express/node_modules/qs
/home/david/Node/chap06/node_modules/mongodb
/home/david/Node/chap06/node_modules/mongoose
/home/david/Node/chap06/node_modules/sqlite3
```

Package scripts

npm allows for package scripts to automatically run at various times in the package lifecycle. Currently there are four lifecycle events: test, start, stop, and restart.

An npm package can include tests which are run as follows:

```
$ npm test <packageName>
```

The start, stop, and restart lifecycle events don't have a defined meaning. An obvious use is starting or stopping daemon processes associated with the package.

Editing and exploring installed package content

npm includes a pair of commands to let you look at or change package content. For example, you could use this during development to read the package source (say, to understand what it's doing), look in the package examples directory, or make modifications to test patches.

For example:

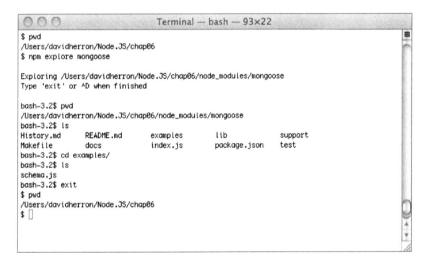

```
$ pwd
/Users/davidherron/Node.JS/chap06
$ npm explore mongoose

Exploring /Users/davidherron/Node.JS/chap06/node_modules/mongoose
Type 'exit' or ^D when finished

bash-3.2$ pwd
/Users/davidherron/Node.JS/chap06/node_modules/mongoose
bash-3.2$ ls
History.md      README.md      examples      lib            support
Makefile        docs           index.js      package.json   test
bash-3.2$ cd examples/
bash-3.2$ ls
schema.js
bash-3.2$ exit
$ pwd
/Users/davidherron/Node.JS/chap06
$ 
```

As the command output implies, the `explore` command spawns a sub-shell whose current directory is the location where the module is installed. Typing exit or *control-D* ends the sub-shell returning you to your login shell.

You can edit files while browsing the package, if you like. If you do, the package may need to be rebuilt as follows:

```
$ npm rebuild mongoose
```

```
mongoose@1.3.3 /home/david/Node/chap06/node_modules/mongoose
```

Updating outdated packages you've installed

The coder codes, updating their package, leaving you in their dust unless you keep up.

To find out if your installed packages are out of date use the following command:

```
$ npm outdated
express@2.3.6 ./node_modules/express current=2.3.3
mongoose@1.3.6 ./node_modules/mongoose current=1.3.3
```

This shows the current installed version as well as the current version in the npm repository. Updating the outdated packages is very simple:

```
$ npm update express
connect@1.4.1 ./node_modules/express/node_modules/connect
mime@1.2.2 ./node_modules/express/node_modules/mime
qs@0.1.0 ./node_modules/express/node_modules/qs
express@2.3.6 ./node_modules/express
```

Uninstalling an installed npm package

It may come to pass that the package of your dreams turns into a nightmare, and even if it does not there are plenty of reasons to remove installed packages. This can be done as follows:

```
$ npm list
/home/david/Node
└── openid@0.1.6
$ npm uninstall openid
$ npm list
/home/david/Node
(empty)
```

Developing and publishing npm packages

Now that we have a good idea of how to use npm let's get to the other end of the process and look at how to develop npm packages. Some of the npm commands serve the development process.

The first step is creating the package.json file, and the npm init command helps you create the initial version. It interrogates you with a few questions and quickly helps you create something like the following:

```
{
  "author": "I.M. Awesome <awesome@example.com>",
  "name": "tmod",
  "description": "Test Module",
  "version": "0.0.1",
  "repository": {
    "url": ""
  },
  "engines": {
    "node": ">0.4.1"
  },
  "dependencies": {},
  "devDependencies": {}
}
```

The next step is obviously to create the package source. npm doesn't have any way to help you with this. You are the coder so you do the coding. Just make sure to keep updating the `package.json` file as you add things to the package. npm does have a couple of commands you'll be using while developing the package.

One of these commands is `npm link`, a lighter-weight method of installing packages. The difference between this and `npm install` is that `npm link` simply sets up a symbolic link to your source directory, and you can freely edit package files without having to repackage and update the package on every change. You can iteratively work on the package, and test it, without having to continually rebuild.

Using `npm link` is a two step process, where first you link your project into the Node installation as follows:

```
$ cd tmod
$ npm link
../../0.4.7/lib/node_modules/tmod -> /home/david/Node/chap03/tmod
```

In the second step you link that package into your application:

```
$ npm link tmod
../node_modules/tmod -> /home/david/Node/0.4.7/lib/node_modules/tmod -> /
home/david/Node/chap03/tmod
```

The arrows (`->`) show you the symbolic link chain that's set up by these commands.

The `npm install` command has a couple of modes that are useful during development. The first is that, if executed in the root of a package directory, it installs the current directory and dependencies into the local `node_modules` directory.

The second is to install tarball's either from a local file or over the network from a URL. Most source code control systems support a URL providing a tarball (compressed tar file) of the source tree. For example, the downloads page on github projects gives a URL like this one:

```
$ npm install https://github.com/havard/node-openid/tarball/v0.1.6
openid@0.1.6 ../node_modules/openid
```

When you're satisfied that your package works, you might want to publish it in the public npm repository so others can use it.

The first step is to register an account with the npm repository. It's done by running the npm adduser command, which asks you a series of questions to establish a username, password, and e-mail address:

```
$ npm adduser
Username: my-user-name
Password:
Email: me@example.com
```

After this step run the npm publish command in the root directory of your package:

```
$ npm publish
```

If all has gone well, after running npm publish, you can go to http://search.npmjs.org and search for the package. It should show up pretty quick.

The npm unpublish command, as the name implies, removes the package from the npm repository.

npm configuration settings

We've already touched on npm configuration earlier with global mode versus local mode. There are a number of other settings to fine-tune npm behavior. Let's first look at the ways to make configuration settings.

First is the npm set and npm get commands, or:

```
npm config set <key> <value> [--global]
npm config get <key>
npm config delete <key>
npm config list
npm config edit
npm get <key>
npm set <key> <value> [--global]
```

For example:

```
$ npm set color true
$ npm set global false
$ npm config get color
true
$ npm config get global
false
```

Environment variables can be used to set configuration values. Any variables which start with NPM_CONFIG_ are interpreted for configuration values. For example, the variable NPM_CONFIG_GLOBAL will set the global configuration value.

Configuration values can be put into configuration files:

- $HOME/.npmrc
- <Node Install Directory>/etc/npmrc

The configuration file contains name=value pairs like the following, and is updated by the npm config set command:

```
$ cat ~/.npmrc
global = false
color = true
```

Package version strings and ranges

Node doesn't know anything about version numbers. It knows about modules, and can treat a directory structure as if it were a module, and it has a fairly rich system of looking for modules, but it doesn't know version numbers. npm however knows about version numbers. It uses the Semantic Versioning model (see further) and as we've seen you can install modules over the Internet, query for out-of-date modules, and update them with npm. All of this is version controlled, so let's take a closer look at the things npm can do with version numbers and version tags.

Earlier we used npm list to list installed packages, and the listing includes version numbers of installed packages. If instead, you wish to see the version number of a specific module, type the following command:

```
$ npm view express version
2.4.0
```

Whenever npm commands take a package name, you can append a version number or version tag to the package name. This way you can deal with specific package versions if needed; for example, if you've tested and qualified your application against a specific version in a staging environment, you can ensure that version is used in the deployment environment:

```
$ npm install express@2.3.1
mime@1.2.2 ./node_modules/express/node_modules/mime
connect@1.5.1 ./node_modules/express/node_modules/connect
qs@0.2.0 ./node_modules/express/node_modules/qs
express@2.3.1 ./node_modules/express
```

npm has a "tag" concept that might be used as shown to install the latest stable release of a package:

```
$ npm install sax@stable
```

Tag names are arbitrary and are not required. The package author designates the tag names and not all packages will use tag names.

Packages list dependencies to other packages in their package.json, which you can view in this way:

```
$ npm view mongoose dependencies
{ hooks: '0.1.9' }


$ npm view express dependencies
{ connect: '>= 1.5.1 < 2.0.0',
  mime: '>= 0.0.1',
  qs: '>= 0.0.6' }
```

The package dependencies is the way npm knows which additional modules to install. When installing a module, it looks at the dependencies and downloads any which are currently not installed.

The sharp-eyed will see the less-than and greater-than signs in this example. npm supports version number ranges, and for example if Express is declaring it will work with any version of Connect between 1.5.1 and 2.0.0.

While this will be straightforward and unsurprising to anybody who has dealt with software at any time, there is a sound model behind the scenes. The npm author used the Semantic Versioning spec at http://semver.org to guide the npm version numbering system. It is as follows:

- Version strings are normally integers arranged as X.Y.Z; X is the Major version, Y is the Minor version, and Z is the Patch (for example, 1.2.3).

- The version string can have an arbitrary text appended immediately after the Patch number for what are called "special versions" (for example, 1.2.3beta1).

- Comparing version strings is not a string comparison, but a numerical comparison of the X, Y, and Z values. For example, 1.9.0 < 1.10.0 < 1.11.3. Further 1.0.0beta1 < 1.0.0beta2 < 1.0.0.

- Compatibility is documented through a version numbering convention:

    ○ Packages with major version 0 (X = 0) are completely unstable and can change any API at any time.

    ○ The Patch number (Z) must be incremented when the only change is backwards-compatible bug fixes.

    ○ The Minor number (Y) must be incremented when backwards-compatible functionality is introduced (for example, a new function, and all other functions remain compatible).

    ○ The Major number (X) must be incremented when incompatible changes are made.

CommonJS modules

Node's module system is based on the the CommonJS module system (http://www.commonjs.org/). While JavaScript is a powerful language with several advanced modern features (such as objects and closures), it lacks a standard object library to facilitate building applications. CommonJS aims to fill that gap with both a convention for implementing modules in JavaScript, and a set of standard modules.

The `require` function takes a module identifier and returns the API exported by the module. If a module requires other modules they are loaded as well. Modules are contained in one JavaScript file, and CommonJS doesn't specify how the module identifier is mapped into a filename.

Modules provide a simple mechanism for encapsulation to hide implementation details while exposing an API. Module content is JavaScript code which is treated as if it were written as follows:

```
(function() { … contents of module file … })();
```

This encapsulates (hides) every top-level object in the module within a private namespace that other code cannot access. This is how the Global Object problem is resolved (more on that shortly).

The exported module API is the object returned by the `require` function. Inside the module it's implemented with a top-level object named `exports` whose fields contain the exported API. To expose a function or object from the module, simply assign it into the `exports` object.

Demonstrating module encapsulation

That was a lot of words, so let's do a quick example. Create a file named `module1.js` containing this:

```
var A = "value A";
var B = "value B";
exports.values = function() {
  return { A: A, B: B };
}
```

Then create a file named `module2.js` containing the following:

```
var util = require('util');
var A = "a different value A";
var B = "a different value B";
var m1 = require('./module1');
util.log('A='+A+' B='+B+' values='+util.inspect(m1.values()));
```

Then run it as follows (you must have already installed Node):

```
$ node module2.js
19 May 21:36:30 - A=a different value A B=a different value B values={ A:
'value A', B: 'value B' }
```

This artificial example demonstrates encapsulation of the values in `module1.js` from those in `module2.js`. The A and B values in `module1.js` don't overwrite A and B in `module2.js`, because they're encapsulated within `module1.js`. Values encapsulated within a module can be exported, such as the `.values` function in `module1.js`.

The Global Object problem mentioned earlier has to do with those variables which are outside the functions, putting them in the global context. In web browsers there is a single global context, and it causes a lot of problems if one JavaScript script steps on the global variables used in another script. With CommonJS modules each module has its own private global context, making it safe to share variables between functions within a module without danger of interfering with global variables in other modules.

Summary

We learned a lot in this chapter about modules and packages for Node.

Specifically, we covered:

- Implementing modules and packages for Node
- Managing installed modules and packages
- How Node locates modules

Now that we've learned about modules and packages, we're ready to use them to build applications, which is the topic of the next chapter.

4
Variations on a Simple Application

Now that we've learned about Node modules it's time to put this knowledge to work in building a simple Node web application. In this chapter, we'll keep the application simple, enabling us to explore three different application frameworks for Node. In later chapters we'll do some more complex applications, but before we can walk we must learn to crawl.

So let's get on with it.

Creating a Math Wizard

The simple and concise application we'll work with in this chapter is a Math Wizard that might, with enough user experience, be useful for teaching mathematics to children. Since we didn't have a user experience expert handy, the Math Wizard application is instead only useful for teaching web application development with Node. Don't expect your children to become math geniuses with this application; you've been warned.

The Math Wizard consists of a home page, a navigation sidebar, and several pages, each of which allows the user to perform mathematical operations.

To use a web framework, or not

Web frameworks help you invest your time in the task without getting lost in the details of implementing HTTP protocol. Abstracting away details is a time honored way for programmers to be more efficient. This is especially true when using a library or framework providing pre-packaged functions that take care of the details.

In this chapter, we'll start by writing an application (called Math Wizard) with no frameworks, then progressively improve it by using Connect and Express.

Implementing the Math Wizard with Node (no frameworks)

We're going to start by crawling, to appreciate what the web frameworks are doing for us. Crawling means starting with Node's core package, the HTTP Server object.

The Math Wizard, like any web application, has multiple pages, each with its own URL. Each page has a few common elements (the general page structure and the navigation bar) and per-page content unique to each page. In the Math Wizard the URLs are as follows:

- `/`: For the wizard's home page
- `/square`: To calculate the square of a number
- `/mult`: To multiply two numbers
- `/factorial`: To calculate the factorial of a number
- `/fibonacci`: To calculate fibonacci numbers

To get started create a directory to hold the source code:

```
$ mkdir chap04
```

Routing requests in Node

Each page of the Math Wizard is implemented with a separate module, with the server routing requests to these modules.

What we mean by "routing requests" is the strategy of splitting the application into multiple modules. Rather than implement every inch of the application in one large callback function, it's best to modularize. Request routing involves code to inspect the incoming HTTP request, then calls the correct modules to handle the request.

Create a file, `app-node.js`, to hold the following:

```
var http_port = 8124;

var http    = require('http');
var htutil  = require('./htutil');

var server = http.createServer(function (req, res) {
  htutil.loadParams(req, res, undefined);
  if (req.requrl.pathname === '/') {
    require('./home-node').get(req, res);
  } else if (req.requrl.pathname === '/square') {
    require('./square-node').get(req, res);
  } else if (req.requrl.pathname === '/factorial') {
    require('./factorial-node').get(req, res);
  } else if (req.requrl.pathname === '/fibonacci') {
    require('./fibo-node').get(req, res);
    // require('./fibo2-node').get(req, res);
  } else if (req.requrl.pathname === '/mult') {
    require('./mult-node').get(req, res);
  } else {
    res.writeHead(404, { 'Content-Type': 'text/plain' });
    res.end("bad URL "+ req.url);
  }
});

server.listen(http_port);
console.log('listening to http://localhost:8124');
```

This request router is straightforward. Each HTTP request invokes this callback with `req` containing data on the request, and `res` used to send back the response. This request router looks at the request URL, and passes the request to a request handling function.

There are several modules, which we'll see in a couple of pages, each of which export a function named `.get` with the the function(req, res) signature, and whose responsibility is to implement one page of the Math Wizard.

If the request URL does not match any of the modules, we send back a 404 status code, the status code for indicating a page not found error.

Handling URL query parameters

The `htutil.loadParams` function helps us out by parsing the URL, and saving the parsed URL object so that the rest of the Math Wizard can refer to it. What's going on is that each page includes a FORM with inputs named a and b. When the user enters numbers and clicks **Submit**, the URL will have a query string that will look like this:

```
http://localhost:8124/mult?a=3&b=7
```

These query parameters will only be there when someone has entered numbers and clicked **Submit**. This means every Math Wizard page must accommodate either case where the parameters exist, or do not. The `htutil.loadParams` function conveniently looks for these parameters saving us from having duplicate code in each module.

Create a file named `htutil.js` containing the following:

```
var url = require('url');
exports.loadParams = function(req, res, next) {
  req.requrl = url.parse(req.url, true);
  req.a = (req.requrl.query.a && !isNaN(req.requrl.query.a))
    ? new Number(req.requrl.query.a)
    : NaN;
  req.b = (req.requrl.query.b && !isNaN(req.requrl.query.b))
    ? new Number(req.requrl.query.b)
    : NaN
    if (next) next();
}
```

This is meant to be called from HTTP request handler functions and to be given the req and res objects received by request handlers. It looks for the a and b query parameters and as already said, attaches them to the req object. The tests, using the `?:` operator, simplifies other code by ensuring that the `req.a` and `req.b` clearly have either the value NaN or a Number, depending on whether a or b query parameters were supplied. There's a function named next which you should ignore for now, because we'll discuss it later when looking at the Connect framework.

The other two functions in `htutil.js` handle page layout. The Math Wizard uses a common layout for each page, and it's best to centralize this to make it easier to change and reduce duplicated code. Later, while using the Express framework we'll use template files for page layout, but in this version of the Math Wizard we're limiting ourselves to the core facilities of Node, which does not include templates.

With `htutil.js` still open, add the following two functions. They are a pair of utility functions to help construct the pages.

```javascript
exports.navbar = function() {
    return ["<div class='navbar'>",
        "<p><a href='/'>home</a></p>",
        "<p><a href='/mult'>Multiplication</a></p>",
        "<p><a href='/square'>Square's</a></p>",
        "<p><a href='/factorial'>Factorial's</a></p>",
        "<p><a href='/fibonacci'>Fibonacci's</a></p>",
        "</div>"].join('\n');
}
```

This function gives us an HTML snippet with links to each page. It will serve as the navigation bar, giving users access to every page.

```javascript
exports.page = function(title, navbar, content) {
    return ["<html><head><title>{title)</title></head>",
        "<body><h1>{title}</h1>",
        "<table><tr>",
        "<td>{navbar}</td><td>{content}</td>",
        "</tr></table></body></html>"
        ].join('\n')
        .replace("{title}", title, "g")
        .replace("{navbar}", navbar, "g")
        .replace("{content}", content, "g");
}
```

This function is the HTML structure for a whole page. It takes arguments to plug the title, the navigation bar, and the content into appropriate sections of the page.

We're using a small trick here with regular expressions and the `replace` function making a clean way to substitute data into a string. The `replace` function is a String function which takes a regular expression, matches it against the string, and replaces the matched text with the supplied string.

In the coming sections we'll see how to use these functions.

Multiplying numbers

Now let's see how to create some mathematics web pages in the Math Wizard. The first is used to multiply numbers (for example, a * b).

Create a file named `mult-node.js` containing then following code:

```javascript
var htutil = require('./htutil');
exports.get = function(req, res) {
  res.writeHead(200, {
    'Content-Type': 'text/html'
  });
```

```
var result = req.a * req.b;
res.end(
  htutil.page("Multiplication", htutil.navbar(), [
    (!isNaN(req.a) && !isNaN(req.b) ?
      ("<p class='result'>{a} * {b} = {result}</p>"
        .replace("{a}", req.a)
        .replace("{b}", req.b)
        .replace("{result}", req.a * req.b))
        : ""),
    "<p>Enter numbers to multiply</p>",
    "<form name='mult' action='/mult' method='get'>",
    "A: <input type='text' name='a' /><br/>",
    "B: <input type='text' name='b' />",
    "<input type='submit' value='Submit' />",
    "</form>"
  ].join('\n'))
);
}
```

The multiplication module, like the other Math Wizard modules, serves two purposes. The first is to display a mathematical result, and the second is to display a form allowing the user to enter one or two values.

The first thing to note is we're using the `htutil.page` function. It provides the overall page layout, and in this function we only provide the main content area of the page. This content is an array of strings which is concatenated using the `.join()` function at the end.

The key part is the following code to display the result, if a parameter was supplied by the user:

```
(!isNaN(req.a) && !isNaN(req.b) ?
  ("<p class='result'>{a} * {b} = {result}</p>"
    .replace("{a}", req.a)
    .replace("{b}", req.b)
    .replace("{result}", req.a * req.b))
    : ""),
```

It uses the `?:` operator to first check if the parameters were supplied, and if so multiply `req.a` and `req.b` and display the result.

Calculating the other mathematical functions

The other Math Wizard modules are similar to `mult-node.js`, using the same general pattern, so let's go through them quickly.

The square of a number is the number multiplied with itself (for example, a * a). Create a file named `square-node.js` containing the following code. Note that we are using Math.floor to ensure rounding req.a to the nearest integer.

```
var htutil = require('./htutil');
exports.get = function(req, res) {
  res.writeHead(200, {
    'Content-Type': 'text/html'
  });
  res.end(
    htutil.page("Square", htutil.navbar(), [
      (!isNaN(req.a) ?
        ("<p class='result'>{a} squared = {sq}</p>"
          .replace("{a}", req.a)
          .replace("{sq}", req.a*req.a))
        : ""),
      "<p>Enter a number to see its square</p>",
      "<form name='square' action='/square' method='get'>",
      "A: <input type='text' name='a' />",
      "</form>"
    ].join('\n'))
  );
}
```

The factorial of an integer n, denoted in mathematics as n!, is the product of n and each positive integer less than n. It's used in many areas of mathematics. Create a file named `factorial-node.js` containing the following code:

```
var htutil = require('./htutil');
var math   = require('./math');

exports.get = function(req, res) {
  res.writeHead(200, {
    'Content-Type': 'text/html'
  });
  res.end(
    htutil.page("Factorial", htutil.navbar(), [
      (!isNaN(req.a) ?
        ("<p class='result'>{a} factorial = {fact}</p>"
          .replace("{a}", req.a)
```

```
        .replace("{fact}",
          math.factorial(Math.floor(req.a))))
      : ""),
      "<p>Enter a number to see it's factorial</p>",
      "<form name='factorial' action='/factorial' method='get'>",
      "A: <input type='text' name='a' />",
      "</form>"
    ].join('\n'))
  );
}
```

Fibonacci numbers are the integers in the following sequence: 0, 1, 1, 2, 3, 5, 8, 13, 21, 34, 55, and so on. Each member of the Fibonacci sequence is the sum of the two previous members in the sequence. The ratio of consecutive elements is approximately equal to the Golden Ratio. Create a file named `fibo-node.js` to contain the page for calculating Fibonacci numbers:

```
var htutil = require('./htutil');
var math   = require('./math');
exports.get = function(req, res) {
  res.writeHead(200, {
    'Content-Type': 'text/html'
  });
  res.end(
    htutil.page("Fibonacci", htutil.navbar(), [
      (!isNaN(req.a) ?
        ("<p class='result'>fibonacci {a} = {fibo}</p>"
          .replace("{a}", Math.floor(req.a))
        .replace("{fibo}", math.fibonacci(Math.floor(req.a))))
        : ""),
      "<p>Enter a number to see its fibonacci</p>",
      "<form name='fibonacci' action='/fibonacci' method='get'>",
      "A: <input type='text' name='a' />",
      "</form>"
    ].join('\n'))
  );
}
```

The sharp-eyed among you will have noticed a module named `math`. It, of course, contains the implementation of a couple of mathematics functions. Create a file named `math.js` containing the following:

```
var factorial = exports.factorial = function(n) {
  if (n == 0)
    return 1;
```

```
      else
        return n * factorial(n-1);
    }

    var fibonacci = exports.fibonacci = function(n) {
      if (n === 1)
        return 1;
      else if (n === 2)
        return 1;
      else
        return fibonacci(n-1) + fibonacci(n-2);
    }
```

These are relatively straightforward implementations of these standard mathematics functions. As we'll see shortly, the Fibonacci function is especially naïve and computationally intensive.

We also want the Math Wizard to have a home page. Create a file named home-node.js containing this code:

```
    var htutil = require('./htutil');
    exports.get = function(req, res) {
      res.writeHead(200, {
        'Content-Type': 'text/html'
      });
      res.end(
        htutil.page("Math Wizard",
          htutil.navbar(),
          "<p>Math Wizard</p>")
      );
    }
```

Enter the following command:

```
$ node app-node.js
```

Since `app-node.js` listens to port 8124, visit `http://localhost:8124/` to see the following:

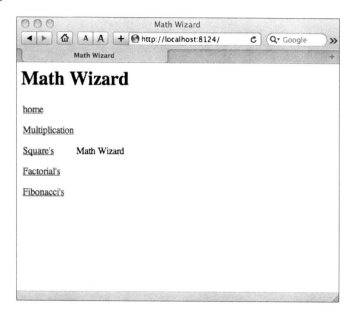

Extending the Math Wizard

Our children need good quality education and maybe this example program is the basis for the best mathematics teaching program ever. Or, maybe not. In any case the Math Wizard can easily be extended with other pages because the world of Mathematics is endless. It's straightforward to add new pages following the pattern already in place using these steps:

- Add an "a" tag in `htutil.navbar`:

  As the `htutil.navbar` function contains the HTML for the navigation bar, any new Math Wizard page needs to be listed there with something like this to list a URL for the page, and the name of the page:

  ```
  "<p><a href='/newUrl'>Math Function Name</a></p>\n"+
  ```

- Add an `if` statement in `app-node.js`:

  Since `app-node.js` contains the request router it, too, needs a new if statement to route the URL we just defined. The URL given here needs to match the one in the `htutil.navbar` function:

  ```
  if (req.requrl.pathname === '/newUrl') {
          require('./moduleName').get(req, res);
  }
  ```

- Add a page handler module which exports a `get` method:

  We've already seen several handler modules (`mult-node.js` and so on), so it's simple to follow these examples to create one.

Long running calculations (fibonacci numbers)

The Math Wizard demonstrates a critical consideration with Node applications. They can bog down if callback functions don't conform to the requirement of quickly returning to the event loop.

To see this, go to the Fibonacci page and enter a "large" number like 50. This will take a LONG time to run (measured in hours or days), the node process will consume a high CPU percentage, and you'll be unable to use the Math Wizard in another browser window. All this is because calculating numbers in the Fibonacci sequence is computationally intensive. Why is the browser unresponsive? This happens because the intense computation prevents the Node event loop from running, preventing Node from responding to browser requests.

Since Node has a single execution thread, processing requests depends on request handlers quickly returning to the event loop. Normally the asynchronous coding style ensures that the event loop executes regularly. This is true even for requests that load data from a server half way around the globe because I/O is non-blocking and control is quickly returned to the event loop. The naïve Fibonacci function we chose doesn't fit into this model, because it's a long running, blocking operation. This type of event handler prevents the system from processing requests and stops Node from doing what it's meant to do, namely to be a blistering fast web server.

In this case, the long-response-time problem is obvious. Response time quickly escalates to the point you can take a vacation to Tibet during the time it takes to respond with the Fibonacci number. Long response times might not be obvious in your application, so how do you know your requests are taking too long? One measurement to make is response latency shown by browser tools such as YSlow. The rule of thumb when there are human beings using a web browser, is to show the next page within a second or two or else run the risk of losing your visitor.

There are two general ways in Node to solve this problem:

- **Algorithmic refactoring**: Perhaps, like the Fibonacci function we chose, one of your algorithms is suboptimal and can be rewritten to be faster. Or, if not faster, to split it into callbacks dispatched through the event loop. We'll look at one such method in a moment.

- **Creating a backend service**: Can you imagine a backend server dedicated to calculating Fibonacci numbers? Okay, maybe not, but it's quite common to implement backend servers to offload work from frontend servers, and we will implement a backend mathematics server at the end of this chapter. The request handler should be making asynchronous calls to data services or databases, assmbling everything required for the response, sending it to the browser when ready.

While we could optimize the Fibonacci algorithm with a less naïve one, we'll instead convert it from a non-asynchronous function to an asynchronous function one with a callback. Using the asynchronous Fibonacci algorithm here isn't the best idea, but it demonstrates the algorithmic refactoring approach. We'll split the calculation into callbacks dispatched through the event loop.

The first thing to do is add a new Fibonacci function to replace the naïve one we originally implemented. This can happen to you as well, that you write a naïve and slow function only to have to replace it with a better one later on. In `math.js` add the following:

```
var fibonacciAsync = exports.fibonacciAsync = function(n, done) {
  if (n === 1 || n === 2)
    done(1);
  else {
    process.nextTick(function() {
      fibonacciAsync(n-1, function(val1) {
        process.nextTick(function() {
          fibonacciAsync(n-2, function(val2) {
            done(val1+val2);
          });
        });
      });
    });
  }
}
```

This is our new asynchronous Fibonacci algorithm. We've converted it from a simple function into an asynchronously driven calculation that sends its result through a callback function like the following:

```
fibonacciAsync(n, function(value) {
    // act on value
});
```

It uses the `process.nextTick` function to convert a recursive function into one whose steps are dispatched through the event loop. This function invokes its callback through the event loop, ensuring the event loop is entered quickly, allowing the server to continue handling HTTP requests. This is not the only method to dispatch steps of an algorithm through the event loop. The async module can do this, and has a long list of functions that help tame asynchronous JavaScript.

In `fibonacciAsync`, `process.nextTick` replaces this statement in the original algorithm:

```
return fibonacci(n-1)+fibonacci(n-2);
```

The task is to calculate the two fibonacci numbers, add them together, and send the result to the caller function. Our new algorithm has three anonymous functions to implement each step of the task. It uses `process.nextTick` to ensure this all happens through the event loop.

Before we go on let's take a moment to ponder on this solution. It does nothing to reduce the computation required; it simply spreads that computation through the event loop. It keeps all the CPU load within the current Node process, and this simply isn't the best way to refactor intense computation like the Fibonacci algorithm. This helps demonstrate dispatching work through the event loop, a technique which will be useful for some algorithms and not so useful for others.

It's up to you, and your specific algorithms, to choose the best method for handling long running computations. For example, later in this chapter we'll demonstrate implementing a backend server, accessed through HTTP, a technique which can send computation elsewhere.

Create a new file, `fibo2-node.js`, and modify `app-node.js` to `require('./fibo2-node')` so it uses the new Fibonacci module. We've already put this line of code in `app-node.js`, but it's commented out. Just change which line is commented out to switch between Fibonacci implementations:

```
var htutil = require('./htutil');
var math  = require('./math');
function sendResult(req, res, a, fiboval) {
  res.writeHead(200, {
    'Content-Type': 'text/html'
  });
  res.end(
    htutil.page("Fibonacci", htutil.navbar(), [
```

```
            (!isNaN(fiboval) ?
              ("<p class='result'>fibonacci {a} = {fibo}</p>"
                .replace("{a}", a)
                .replace("{fibo}", fiboval))
            : ""),
            "<p>Enter a number to see its fibonacci</p>",
            "<form name='fibonacci' action='/fibonacci' method='get'>",
            "A: <input type='text' name='a' />",
            "</form>"
        ].join('\n'))
    );
}


exports.get = function(req, res) {
    if (!isNaN(req.a)) {
        math.fibonacciAsync(Math.floor(req.a), function(val) {
            sendResult(req, res, Math.floor(req.a), val);
        });
    } else {
        sendResult(req, res, NaN, NaN);
    }
}
```

We've refactored this from the original by moving the work to a function, sendResult, which we call in two different ways depending on whether or not there is a Fibonacci number to display.

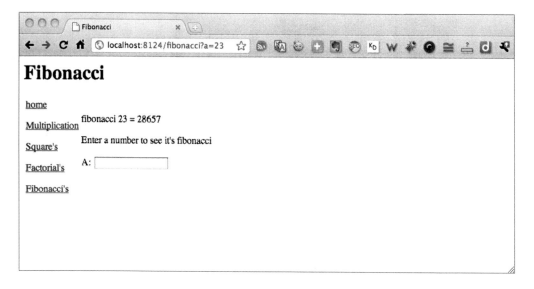

Large Fibonacci number requests still take a long time to calculate, but the server isn't blocked and can handle other requests. You can easily see this by opening multiple browser tabs. In one tab request a large Fibonacci number that will take a long time to compute. In another tab make other requests. As you see in this screenshot, rather than unresponsive boringness it handles your requests.

What "complete web server" features are missing?

As we'll see later when discussing Connect, the rather minimal `dispatch` function in the Math Wizard does not do several things that real web servers do. Just implementing the HTTP protocol does not make a complete web server or web application because it's missing several useful best practices developed over the last 20 years of web application development:

- The Math Wizard application doesn't look at the request method (`GET`, `PUT`, `POST`, and so on). Maintaining HTTP semantics requires behaving differently for `GET`, `PUT`, or `POST` requests.

- It doesn't provide a page for bad URLs (the 404 page).

- Neither the URL nor the forms are screened for any injected scripting attacks.

- It doesn't support handling cookies, nor does it use cookies to maintain sessions.

- It doesn't log requests.

- It doesn't support authentication.

- It doesn't handle static files such as images, CSS, JavaScript, or HTML.

- It doesn't limit anything such as page size, or execution time.

As we'll see later with Connect and Express, the Node web frameworks provide most of these missing features.

Using Connect to implement the Math Wizard

Connect (`http://senchalabs.github.com/connect/`) is not described as a web framework, but instead as a middleware framework for Node. It ships with "11 bundled middleware" and there is "a rich choice of third-party middleware". It's okay if you're confused by the term "middleware" since it's such a general word; so let's start by closely examining that word.

TJ Holowaychuck has described "middleware" as providing Node developers with simple "plug-and-play" modules, which can be "stacked" in any order, and aid in rapid application development providing useful common web application functionality such as request routing, authentication, request logging, cookie handling, and more (`http://tjholowaychuk.com/post/664516126/connect-middleware-for-nodejs`).

Middleware comes in two flavors:

- **filters**: Sit in the middle of the request flow processing incoming and outgoing traffic but not themselves responding to requests. An example of a filter is the "*logger*" middleware which provides customizable logging.
- **providers**: Are "*end-points*" in the stack, meaning that an incoming request stops at a provider, and it's the provider which sends the response. An example of a provider is the "*static*" middleware which serves static files.

In the previous section, we saw an application built using `http.createServer` and a function that is called for each HTTP request arriving on the server. With Connect you instead use `connect.createServer` and then attach middleware modules to that server. One of the middleware modules, router, is used to implement application URLs.

With that in mind, let's look at some code.

Installing Connect and other setup

First, make sure that Connect is installed:

```
$ npm install connect
```

Now, create the file `app-connect.js` with this content:

```
var connect = require('connect');
var htutil  = require('./htutil');

connect.createServer()
  .use(connect.favicon())
  .use(connect.logger())
  .use('/filez', connect.static(__dirname + '/filez'))
  .use(connect.router(function(app){
    app.get('/',
      require('./home-node').get);
    app.get('/square', htutil.loadParams,
      require('./square-node').get);
    app.get('/factorial', htutil.loadParams,
```

```
        require('./factorial-node').get);
      app.get('/fibonacci', htutil.loadParams,
        require('./fibo2-node').get);
      app.get('/mult', htutil.loadParams,
        require('./mult-node').get);
    })).listen(8124);
  console.log('listening to http://localhost:8124');
```

Then execute the server as follows:

$ node app-connect.js

Since the server is started with .listen(8124), visit `http://localhost:8124/` in your web browser.

Congratulations! We have now just run our first Connect based Node application.

You'll notice it behaves and looks exactly like the previous incarnation of the Math Wizard. This is because `app-connect.js` reuses modules from `app-node.js`. The `app.get` functions simply passes requests to one of the existing modules.

If it's behaving the same then what's the big deal?

The difference is that Connect offers a request processing and dispatch framework to ease application development. It takes care of many of the "complete web server" features mentioned earlier, letting you focus more on your application. But does this make it an application framework?

Connect isn't presented as an application framework but as the basis upon which to build an application framework. Express is one such application framework built upon Connect. Connect is useful by itself, and understanding Connect helps to understand Express, so we'll have a short discussion of Connect and then move on to Express.

Connecting with Connect

We've just had a taste of Connect so let's take a more careful look. Connect is the basis for the Express framework, and it resolves practically all of the limitations discussed earlier with applications built on the HTTP Server object. Before we get ahead of ourselves, let's take a look at `app-connect.js`.

In Connect there are several ways of setting up and configuring the server object. The way we're doing it in `app-connect.js` is as follows:

```
var connect = require('connect');
connect.createServer()
```

```
.use(connect.favicon())
.use(connect.logger())
.use('/filez', connect.static(__dirname + '/filez'))
.use(connect.router(function(app){
  // configure the router
})).listen( .. port number ..);
```

The `.use` method is one way to attach middleware to a Connect server. This sets up a series of middleware modules invoked on every request. The middleware modules to use of course, depend on your application.

The `.use` method allows one to chain `.use` invocations for a nicer programming experience (`server.use().use().use().use()`).

In this case we're configuring the *favicon*, *logger*, *static*, and *router* middleware.

The logger middleware is useful for creating an Apache style access log. By default it prints to the terminal but can be configured to print in any format or to any file.

The static middleware implements a "static web server" to deliver the files located under the specified directory. What that means is if you have a directory hierarchy containing `.html` or `.css` or `.js` files to send to browsers, the `connect.static` middleware will do the job.

Favicons are those little images which some web browsers show in the location bar, on tabs, and are generally another little place for your branding to exist, and the favicon middleware handles it for you.

The router middleware serves the purpose of directing requests for each URL to the correct handler function. It's configuration starts with the following :

```
.use(connect.router(function(app){
  // configure the router
})
```

But the real power here is the router configuration code where you declare the URLs recognized by the application, and the handler function for each URL. The pattern for router configuration is as follows:

```
app.requestName('path', function(req, res, next) {..});
```

The *requestName* is one of the HTTP verbs such as `get`, `put`, `post`, and so on. This means you can have an HTML form on a page, and with `method=POST`, use an `app.get` function to send the page to the browser, and use an `app.post` function to receive posted requests on this form. We'll see an example in *Chapter 6, Data Storage and Retrieval* but it might look like the following, assuming appropriately defined functions:

```
app.get('/form', createPageWithForm);
app.post('/form', receiveValuesPostedWithForm);
```

The callback function have one more function argument than the usual request handler. Its signature is `function(req, res, next)` where `req` and `res` have the usual meaning of HTTP Request and HTTP Response. The `next` argument is a function provided by Connect which plays a role in making sure that all middleware functions are executed.

Routes can dispatch to multiple functions, as we do in `app-connect.js`. Connect will call each function in turn so long as the `next` function is used. In `app-connect.js` we are using `htutil.loadParams`, as we did in `app-node.js`. You'll remember that this includes use of a function named `next`, which we now know is provided by Connect.

Here's a typical router configuration function:

```
app.get('/square', htutil.loadParams,
    require('./square-node').get);
```

The arguments are a URL string and two functions, the first being `htutil.loadParams`. Router configuration functions can contain any number of functions like this and you can construct the series of processing functions needed for your application.

Taken together the middleware and multiple router functions are a kind of state machine for processing HTTP requests. We've seen that there are two series of functions. The first is the middleware functions listed in the server configuration, and the second is the list of router functions we've just looked at.

Using Express to implement the Math Wizard

Now that we understand Connect, let's take the Math Wizard on its next evolutionary step with Express. Express is a web application framework built upon Connect (a middleware framework). This means that the focus of Express is on constructing an application, including providing a template system, where the focus of Connect is on web server infrastructure. The same team develops both Express and Connect so it shouldn't be surprising to learn the APIs are extremely similar.

For example, this is Hello World in Express:

```
var app = require('express').createServer();
app.get('/', function(req, res) {
  res.send('Hello, world!');
});
app.listen(3000);
```

This should look similar to the code for Connect we went over in the previous section. However, the object returned from `createServer` has the router middleware functions attached to it. The feeling is very much as if you're skipping past most of the middleware attaching and configuring, and instead going direct for the URL router. You can still attach and configure middleware, of course:

```
var express = require('express');
var app = express.createServer(
  express.logger(),
  express.bodyParser()
);
```

To install Express and EJS (a template processing system) simply do the following :

```
$ npm install express ejs
qs@0.1.0 ../node_modules/express/node_modules/qs
express@2.3.11 ../node_modules/express
ejs@0.4.2 ../node_modules/ejs
```

Implementing the Express Math Wizard

With the required modules installed let's start coding. To prepare for coding the Express Math Wizard, create a directory:

```
$ mkdir views
```

And create the file `app-express.js` containing the following:

```
var htutil  = require('./htutil');
var math   = require('./math');
var express = require('express');
var app = express.createServer(
  express.logger()
);

app.register('.html', require('ejs'));
// Optional since express defaults to CWD/views
app.set('views', __dirname + '/views');
```

```
app.set('view engine', 'ejs');

app.configure(function(){
  app.use(app.router);
  app.use(express.static(__dirname + '/filez'));
  app.use(express.errorHandler({
    dumpExceptions: true, showStack: true }));
});
```

This sets up the server and configures the required middleware. Some of the details are different, for example, `express.logger` rather than `connect.logger`, but everything should look familiar.

Among the new things are `app.register` and `app.set`. The configuration shown here configures the template system so that `.html` files are processed by the EJS engine. We'll see in a moment how `res.render` is used to render data into templates through one of several template engines.

Now for the router configuration (still in `app-express.js`):

```
app.get('/', function(req, res) {
  res.render('home.html', { title: "Math Wizard" });
});
app.get('/mult', htutil.loadParams, function(req, res) {
  if (req.a && req.b) req.result = req.a * req.b;
  res.render('mult.html', {
    title: "Math Wizard" , req: req });
});
app.get('/square', htutil.loadParams, function(req, res) {
  if (req.a) req.result = req.a * req.a;
  res.render('square.html', {
    title: "Math Wizard" , req: req });
});
app.get('/fibonacci', htutil.loadParams, function(req, res) {
  if (req.a) {
    math.fibonacciAsync(Math.floor(req.a), function(val) {
      req.result = val;
      res.render('fibo.html', {
        title: "Math Wizard" , req: req });
    });
  } else {
    res.render('fibo.html', {
      title: "Math Wizard" , req: req });
  }
});
```

```
app.get('/factorial', htutil.loadParams, function(req, res) {
  if (req.a) req.result = math.factorial(req.a);
  res.render('factorial.html', {
    title: "Math Wizard" , req: req });
});

app.get('/404', function(req, res) {
  res.send('NOT FOUND '+req.url);
});

app.listen(8124);
console.log('listening to http://localhost:8124');
```

Router configuration in Express is largely the same as for Connect, except filtered through a parallel universe. As already noted, the router functions are directly available on the server object. The main difference is in what we're doing in the router functions because of template engine support.

In Express we send pages using the res.render function rather than res.writeHead and res.end, as we did before. The res.render function renders data through a template file, letting us implement some healthy separation between presentation and code.

EJS is just one of the template systems available in Express. Our configuration is to use it for any file within the views directory with the .html extension.

There are other template engines, and lacking configuration the file extension is used to indicate the template engine as follows:

```
res.render('index.haml', {..data..}); // Use Haml
res.render('index.jade', {..data..}); // Use Jade
res.render('index.ejs', {..data..}); // Use EJS
res.render('index.coffee', {..data..}); // Use CoffeeKup
res.render('index.jqtpl', {..data..}); // Use jQueryTemplates
```

You can also change the default rendering engine with app.set as follows:

```
app.set('view engine', 'haml'); // Use Haml
app.set('view engine', 'jade'); // Use Jade
app.set('view engine', 'ejs'); // Use EJS
```

Now that we've talked about the code, let's create the template files. They are all to be placed in the views directory.

First, in `layout.html` let's add the following code:

```html
<html>
  <head><title><%= title %></title></head>
  <body>
    <h1><%= title %></h1>
    <table>
      <tr><td>
          <div class='navbar'>
            <p><a href='/'>home</a></p>
            <p><a href='/mult'>Multiplication</a></p>
            <p><a href='/square'>Square's</a></p>
            <p><a href='/factorial'>Factorial's</a></p>
            <p><a href='/fibonacci'>Fibonacci's</a></p>
          </div>
        </td>
        <td><%- body %></td>
      </tr>
    </table></body></html>
```

In Express the `layout` template is special. You'll note that in `app.js` we used `res.render('fibo.html' .. )` and nowhere was `layout.html` mentioned. What's going on? The default behavior is for the rendered contents of the named template to be passed on to the `layout` template as the variable named `body`. When `app.js` calls `res.render('fibo.html' .. )` it first renders a page snippet with `fibo.html`, then renders the whole page using the `layout` template.

There are two ways to override this default behavior. The first is to make a global setting in Express that turns off (or on) all use of the `layout` template:

```
app.set('view options', { layout: false (or true) });
```

The second way is to override the `layout` template for a specific rendering:

```
res.render('myview.ejs', { layout: false (or true) });
```

To disable (or enable) the `layout` template on a specific rendering, or to use a different `layout` template use the following:

```
res.render('page', { layout: 'mylayout.jade' });
```

EJS templates are mostly HTML except for three special kinds of tags. These should be familiar if you've used other template systems:

- Unbuffered code for conditionals and so on <% code %>
- Escapes html by default with <%= code %>
- Unescaped buffering with <%- code %>

We see here the use of escaped HTML, with `<%= title %>`, and unbuffered data, with the `<%- body %>` tag.

Let's get back to the Math Wizard templates next, `home.html`:

```
<p>Math Wizard</p>
```

And, that's it.

In `mult.html` we will add the following code:

```
<% if (req.a && req.b) { %>
  <p class='result'>
    <%= req.a %> * <%= req.b %> = <%= req.result %>
  </p>
<% } %>
<p>Enter numbers to multiply</p>
<form name='mult' action='/mult' method='get'>
  A: <input type='text' name='a' /><br/>
  B: <input type='text' name='b' />
  <input type='submit' value='Submit' />
</form>
```

Here we see the use of `<% code %>` tags to introduce a bit of conditional rendering of the appropriate bits if we have data to render:

```
<% if (req.a && req.b) { %>
  conditional content
<% } %>
```

The code within `<% code %>` tags is JavaScript to do anything, however in this case we're using an `if` statement to conditionally render some content. If you were to have a list or array of data you might use a `while` statement to loop over and render the items.

Now in `square.html` we'll add the following code:

```
<% if (req.a) { %>
  <p class='result'>
    <%= req.a %> squared = <%= req.result %>
```

```
  </p>
<% } %>
<p>Enter numbers to multiply</p>
<form name='square' action='/square' method='get'>
  A: <input type='text' name='a' />
  <input type='submit' value='Submit' />
</form>
```

Now in `factorial.html` we'll add the following code:

```
<% if (req.a) { %>
 <p class='result'>
    <%= req.a %> factorial = <%= req.result %>
 </p>
<% } %>
<p>Enter a number to see it's factorial</p>
<form name='factorial' action='/factorial' method='get'>
  A: <input type='text' name='a' />
  <input type='submit' value='Submit' />
</form>
```

And finally, in `fibo.html` we'll add the following code:

```
<% if (req.a) { %>
  <p class='result'>
    fibonacci <%= req.a %> = <%= req.result %>
  </p>
<% } %>
<p>Enter a number to see it's fibonacci</p>
<form name='fibonacci' action='/fibonacci' method='get'>
  A: <input type='text' name='a' />
  <input type='submit' value='Submit' />
</form>
```

Now, with all that set up you can run the application using the following:

```
$ node app-express.js
```

Then visit the application in your browser at `http://localhost:8124/` and enjoy the Math Wizard.

Handling errors

Errors will happen. It's best to learn about errors early because early detection makes it cheaper to fix errors. Express provides two ways to catch errors.

In the Math Wizard we had this line of code:

```
app.use(express.errorHandler({
  dumpExceptions: true, showStack: true
}));
```

This is the default error handler and shows a geek-friendly, developer-friendly stack trace. It's not what you want to show to real visitors. Instead you might want to show something like a whale being lifted out of the ocean by a flock of birds. The first step to showing user-friendly errors is to install a handler for error events using the `app.error` function. Note the function it takes has an additional parameter, `err`, which contains the error object:

```
app.error(function(err, req, res, next) {
// ...
  res.send(... error page); // or res.render('template'..)
});
```

This is where your brilliance can shine with a fun error page, or maybe you'll instead make yet another dull, boring error page. It's up to you.

Parameterized URLs and data services

So far we've looked at applications that send HTML to a web browser. While that's an important use case, Express (and Connect) can be used for many other things. For example, we commonly use HTTP to build REST services to send data meant to be consumed by an application rather than HTML meant for human enjoyment.

Earlier we pondered (and dismissed) the likelihood of a Fibonacci server to offload Fibonacci calculations from the frontend web server to a backend. Let's go ahead and build one, just to see the basics of how to do it. Along the way we'll take a look at Express's parameterized routing feature, and formatting a response as data. So let's get started.

Parametrized URLs in Express

The routing system in express allows your URL to specify placeholders that become available in the `req` object. It can make your program more flexible than non-parameterized URLs. It's done by a kind of pattern matching with tokens plugged into URL elements. Express examines the request URL, matching it against the patterns you specify, extracting matching elements from the URL, and filling the data into fields in the `req` object.

An example might make this clearer:

```
app.get('/user/:id', function(req, res){
  res.send('user ' + req.params.id);
});
```

In the URL, `/user/:id` has a placeholder token named `id`. Express recognizes the stuff after `/user/` and assigns it to the `req.params.id` field. The pattern can be a regular expression, if you prefer.

The mathematics server (and client)

Now let's create a simple server for supporting mathematics calculations, returning the results through a JSON object. It'll support the same four operations we had in the Math Wizard.

Create a file named `math-server.js` containing the following:

```
var math  = require('./math');
var express = require('express');
var app = express.createServer(
  //express.logger()
);
app.configure(function(){
  app.use(app.router);
  app.use(express.errorHandler({
    dumpExceptions: true, showStack: true }));
});

app.get('/fibonacci/:n', function(req, res, next) {
  math.fibonacciAsync(Math.floor(req.params.n),
  function(val) {
    res.send({ n: req.params.n, result: val });
  });
});
app.get('/factorial/:n', function(req, res, next) {
  res.send({
```

```
      n: req.params.n,
      result: math.factorial(Math.floor(req.params.n))
    });
  });
  app.get('/mult/:a/:b', function(req, res, next) {
    res.send({
      a: req.params.a, b: req.params.b,
      result: req.params.a * req.params.b
    });
  });
  app.get('/square/:a', function(req, res, next) {
    res.send({
      a: req.params.a,
      result: req.params.a * req.params.a
    });
  });
  app.listen(3002);
```

That's the entire server, except for the math module, which is the same one we used earlier. It has a slightly stripped down configuration, and is set up to listen on `http://localhost:3002/` so that it can be used as the backend of the Math Wizard.

The routes we specify are straightforward, providing space for the function arguments needed for each operation.

This is the first time we've seen `res.send` used. It's a flexible way to send responses which can take an array of header values (for the HTTP response header), and an HTTP status code. As used here it automatically detects the object, formats it as JSON text, and sends it with the correct Content-Type.

Now let's run it:

```
$ node math-server.js &
[1] 10483
$ curl -f http://localhost:3002/square/34.2
{"a":"34.2","result":1169.64}
$ curl -f http://localhost:3002/mult/3.3/3
{"a":"3.3","b":"3","result":9.899999999999999}
$ curl -f http://localhost:3002/factorial/20
{"n":"20","result":2432902008176640000}
$ curl -f http://localhost:3002/fibonacci/20
{"n":"20","result":6765}
```

Now that we've implemented a server, what about the client?

Because this is an HTTP service, client programs make HTTP requests to the server. Node includes an excellent HTTP Client object, and in *Chapter 5, A Simple Web Server, EventEmitters, and HTTP Clients* we'll look at it in more depth.

The task is to construct an HTTP request, send the request, wait for the response, decode the response body, and make use of it. While you can do this in a web application like the Math Wizard, let's make a simple terminal client application to the math server.

Create a file named `math-client.js` containing the following:

```
var http = require('http');
var util = require('util');
[
  "/fibonacci/20", "/factorial/20",
  "/mult/10/20", "/square/12"
].forEach(function(path) {
  var req = http.request({
    host: "localhost",
    port: 3002,
    path: path,
    method: 'GET'
  }, function(res) {
    res.on('data', function (chunk) {
      util.log('BODY: ' + chunk);
    });
  });
  req.end();
});
```

The code `http.request` creates an HTTP request, but with the URL elements split out into the parameters object. We'll go deeper into this in the next chapter, but what you need to know right now is that the callback declared in the `res.on` statement is triggered when the HTTP response data arrives.

Hence `math-client.js` makes a few hardcoded requests against the `math-server.js`, printing out the results as follows:

```
$ node math-client.js
7 Jun 22:17:49 - BODY: {"n":"20","result":2432902008176640000}
7 Jun 22:17:49 - BODY: {"a":"12","result":144}
7 Jun 22:17:49 - BODY: {"a":"10","b":"20","result":200}
7 Jun 22:17:49 - BODY: {"n":"20","result":6765}
```

The sharp-eyed among you will have noticed the responses arrived out of order from how they're listed in the array. The response for the Fibonacci request arrived last, while having been requested first. Recall that callbacks occur asynchronously based on when they arrive in the event loop, and that the Fibonacci function can take a while to calculate its result. What happened is that calculating the 20th element of the Fibonacci series took a long time. In `math-client.js` the requests are all sent very quickly, because its work to send requests is very small, and the printout we see here is a result of invoking the `res.on('data'..)` handlers. Answering the request in `math-server.js` is an `app.get` request handler. Each `res.on('data'..)` handler is tied to an `app.get request` handler invocation through the socket over which the HTTP request was made. When an `app.get` request handler calls `res.send`, its HTTP response in turn causes the `res.on('data'..)` handler waiting for that response to be invoked.

What determines the ordering of which result is printed first? It's the length of time `math-server.js` spends calculating each result, because the result is printed only after the response arrives.

In most cases the calculation is quick (a multiplication) and it returns the answer almost immediately. The Fibonacci query, as we discussed before, is a different story. Since `fibonacciAsync` is used, calculation of Fibonacci values will happen in parallel with calculating the other responses and the 20th Fibonacci number takes enough time to calculate that the other values were calculated first, and arrived first in the client. Changing the Fibonacci request value to 2 changes it to a shorter calculation, changing the arrival order of the responses, as we see here:

```
$ node math-client.js
7 Jun 22:34:49 - BODY: {"n":"2","result":1}
7 Jun 22:34:49 - BODY: {"a":"10","b":"20","result":200}
7 Jun 22:34:49 - BODY: {"n":"20","result":2432902008176640000}
7 Jun 22:34:49 - BODY: {"a":"12","result":144}
```

Refactoring Math Wizard to use math server

Now that we have this client function, it's a fairly simple matter to transplant it into a request handler in the Math Wizard. Earlier we pondered how to keep the frontend user-facing server handling requests for happy users, while at the same time hosting a potentially heavy-weight calculation. Calculating members of the Fibonacci sequence is an example of a heavy-weight calculation that, if performed on a user-facing server, could detract from user happiness.

The solution we looked at before was refactoring the algorithm to split its calculations into chunks distributed through the event queue. While this strategy will work in some cases it does mean the user-facing server is still performing the calculation, and the refactored algorithm may be less efficient than before. With `math-client.js` we have yet another way to solve this problem, sending the work to a backend server or maybe a load-balanced cluster of servers.

In `app-express.js` replace the `/fibonacci` request handler with the following:

```
app.get('/fibonacci', htutil.loadParams, function(req, res) {
  if (req.a) {
    var httpreq = require('http').request({
      host: "localhost",
      port: 3002,
      path: "/fibonacci/"+Math.floor(req.a),
      method: 'GET'
    }, function(httpresp) {
      httpresp.on('data', function (chunk) {
        var data = JSON.parse(chunk);
        req.result = data.result;
        res.render('fibo.html',
          { title: "Math Wizard", req: req });
      });
    });
    httpreq.end();
    //math.fibonacciAsync(Math.floor(req.a), function(val) {
      //req.result = val;
      //res.render('fibo.html',
        //{ title: "Math Wizard" , req: req });
    //});
  } else {
    res.render('fibo.html',
      { title: "Math Wizard" , req: req });
  }
});
```

What's happening is this new request handler is itself turning around and making an HTTP request from the backend server we just implemented (`math-server.js`). In effect this is the simplest of REST style backend services you can imagine. The backend server defines several URLs for HTTP GET requests, it returns JSON with the data, and our request handler parses that JSON to get the result.

You run this the same way, after modifying the request handler function:

```
$ node app-express.js
```

Again, it behaves the same as if you're using `fibonacciAsync`, so what's the big deal? Why would you architect the use of any backend service? For the Math Wizard this is probably overkill, but it demonstrates a commonly made choice which could be perfect for your application. Here are a few reasons to consider:

- It may be best to remove heavy computation demands from the frontend user-facing server, leaving it free to interact with web browsers.
- Load balancing to distribute requests over multiple servers (cloud computing).
- Responses from `math-server.js` are deterministic making a caching proxy an attractive way to get a dramatic speed boost. Why recalculate answers that have already been answered?
- It lets you use fancy buzzwords to impress your boss.

The ease with which we implemented `math-server.js` and integrated it into the Math Wizard demonstrates all over again the simplicity and power Node brings to the game.

Summary

We learned a lot in this chapter, and are now ready to start writing some real applications. But first let's recap what we covered:

- Request handling and modularization into separate modules
- Creating web applications with the HTTP Server object, and with the Connect and Express frameworks
- Handling URL query parameters from FORM submissions
- The impact of long running calculations on server responsiveness and user happiness, as well as methods to fix it
- Using the async module to tame asynchronous coding practices
- Some aspects of a full web application stack provided by Connect and Express
- What Connect means by middleware
- How to handle different HTTP verbs with Connect and Express routing rules

- Using parameterized URL's in Express
- Implementing a REST style backend server to distribute computation load

Now that we've learned so much about implementing web applications let's take a closer look at the HTTP server and client objects and the events distributing system in Node.

5

A Simple Web Server, EventEmitters, and HTTP Clients

Now that we've seen how to create Node applications using the Express web framework, let's dig under the covers into the details of HTTP web server implementation. In this chapter, we'll implement a simple web server that supplies a few of the attributes of real web servers discussed in *Chapter 4, Variations on a Simple Application*.

It's generally best to let the web application framework take care of details, because the HTTP protocol is complex to implement correctly. So why do we want to implement our own HTTP web server? There are several reasons as follows:

- Understanding why to choose one framework or another
- Understanding why a framework does what it does
- Not every task fits into the opinions embedded in a framework design
- Sometimes you need to code directly to the bare HTTP layer to implement web services rather than web applications
- Maybe you have a better idea than the framework authors

Let's get started.

Sending and receiving events with EventEmitters

The EventEmitter object is a key part of using Node to implement applications, but it's so much a part of the woodwork that you may miss its existence. Many of Node's objects subclass from EventEmitter, using its methods to send events to signal certain conditions. These events go through Node's event loop, eventually invoking callback functions.

In this chapter, we'll be working with the HTTPServer and HTTPClient objects. Both of them subclass EventEmitter and rely on it to send events for each step of the HTTP protocol. Understanding EventEmitter will help you understand not only these objects but many other objects in Node.

The EventEmitter object is defined in Node's events module. Directly using the EventEmitter class means doing require('events'), but this is not required except for cases which explicitly need you to. The many objects in Node that use EventEmitter do so without requiring you to call require('events').

This example (pulser.js) shows both sending and receiving events while directly using the EventEmitter class:

```
var events = require('events');
var util   = require('util');

function Pulser() {
  events.EventEmitter.call(this);
}
util.inherits(Pulser, events.EventEmitter);

Pulser.prototype.start = function() {
  var self = this;
  this.id = setInterval(function() {
    util.log('>>>> pulse');
    self.emit('pulse');
    util.log('<<<< pulse');
  }, 1000);
}
```

This defines a class, Pulser, which inherits from EventEmitter (using util. inherits). Its purpose is to send timed events, once a second, to any listeners. The start method uses setInterval to kick off repeated callback execution, scheduled for every second, and calling emit to send pulse events to any listeners.

This much of `pulser.js` could be a standalone module for any application needing timer events at regularly scheduled intervals.

Now let's see how to use the `Pulser` object:

```
var pulser = new Pulser();
pulser.on('pulse', function() {
  util.log('pulse received');
});
pulser.start();
```

Here we create a `Pulser` object, and consume its `pulse` events. Calling `pulser.on('pulse'..)` sets up connections for `pulse` events to invoke the callback function. It then calls the `start` method to get the process going.

Having entered this into a file named `pulser.js`, run it, and you should see the following output:

```
$ node pulser.js
23 May 20:30:20 - >>>> pulse
23 May 20:30:20 - pulse received
23 May 20:30:20 - <<<< pulse
23 May 20:30:21 - >>>> pulse
23 May 20:30:21 - pulse received
23 May 20:30:21 - <<<< pulse
...
```

EventEmitter theory

EventEmitter events are named, such as the `pulse` event used here. Event names can be anything which makes sense to you and you can define as many events as you like. Event names are defined simply by calling `.emit` with the event name. There's nothing formal to do, no registry of event names, and simply making a call to `.emit` is enough to define an event name. By convention, the event name `error` indicates errors.

An object sends events using the `.emit` function. Events are sent to any listeners which have registered to receive events from the object. The program does so by calling that object's `.on` method, giving the event name, as well as a callback function to receive the event.

We can see this in `pulse.js`. The `Pulser` object calls `self.emit('pulse')` to send events, and later in the file, `pulse.on('pulse', ..)` is called to receive those events.

Often it is required to send data along with an event. To do so, simply add the data as arguments to the `.emit` call, as follows:

```
self.emit('eventName', data1, data2, ..);
```

Then when the program receives that event, the data appears as arguments to the callback function. Your program would listen to such an event as follows:

```
emitter.on('eventName', function(data1, data2, ..) {
  // act on event
});
```

We'll see some practical examples of this with the HTTP objects beginning in the next section. All of the HTTP client and server objects are EventEmitters sending events correlating with different stages of the HTTP protocol. For example, every incoming HTTP request is encapsulated in a `Request` object. The `Request` object sends `data` events as request data arrives, sends an `end` event when all data has arrived, and sends a `close` event if the socket closes before the `end` event was sent.

HTTP Sniffer—listening to the HTTP conversation

Now let's start working with the HTTP objects by creating a useful class which listens to all events emitted by an HTTP Server object. It could be a useful debugging tool which also demonstrates how HTTP server objects operate.

Node's HTTP Server object is an EventEmitter and the HTTP Sniffer simply listens to every server event, printing out information pertinent to each event.

Create a file named `httpsniffer.js` containing the following:

```
var util = require('util');
var url  = require('url');

exports.sniffOn = function(server) {
  server.on('request', function(req, res) {
    util.log('e_request');
    util.log(reqToString(req));
  });

  server.on('close', function(errno) {
    util.log('e_close errno='+ errno);
  });
```

```
    server.on('checkContinue', function(req, res) {
      util.log('e_checkContinue');
      util.log(reqToString(req));
      res.writeContinue();
    });

    server.on('upgrade', function(req, socket, head) {
      util.log('e_upgrade');
      util.log(reqToString(req));
    });

    server.on('clientError', function() {
      util.log('e_clientError');
    };

    // server.on('connection', ..);
  }

  var reqToString = function(req) {
    var ret = 'request ' + req.method +' '+
      req.httpVersion +' '+ req.url +'\n';
    ret += JSON.stringify(url.parse(req.url, true)) +'\n';
    var keys = Object.keys(req.headers);
    for (var i = 0, l = keys.length; i < l; i++) {
      var key = keys[i];
      ret += i +' '+ key +': '+ req.headers[key] +'\n';
    }
    if (req.trailers)
      ret += req.trailers +'\n';
      return ret;
  }
  exports.reqToString = reqToString;
```

That was a lot of code, but the key to it is the sniffOn function. When given an
HTTP Server function, it uses the .on function to connect listener functions that print
data about each event emitted by the HTTP Server object. The events for this object
correspond to the HTTP protocol exchanges the server makes with its client.

An example of using the HTTP Sniffer is this modified version of the simple hello world server (`hwserver.js`):

```
var http    = require('http');
var sniffer = require('./httpsniffer');

var server = http.createServer(function (req, res) {
  res.writeHead(200, {'Content-Type': 'text/plain'});
  res.end('Hello, World!\n');
});
sniffer.sniffOn(server);
server.listen(3000);
```

With this in place, upon running the following server:

```
$ node hwserver.js
```

you can visit `http://localhost:3000/` in your browser and see the following console output. Notice that two requests are made, one for / and one for `/favicon.ico`. The Favicon is that little image some browsers show to help you brand your website. The server we're using at this moment doesn't support this file but we'll see later how to implement it.

```
$ node hwserver.js

6 Apr 21:14:38 - e_request

6 Apr 21:14:38 - request GET 1.1 /

{"search":"","query":{},"pathname":"/","href":"/"}

0 host: localhost:3000

1 user-agent: Mozilla/5.0 (Macintosh; U; Intel Mac OS X 10_6_7; en-us)
AppleWebKit/533.20.25 (KHTML, like Gecko) Version/5.0.4 Safari/533.20.27

2 accept: application/xml,application/xhtml+xml,text/html;q=0.9,text/
plain;q=0.8,image/png,*/*;q=0.5

3 cache-control: max-age=0

4 accept-language: en-us

5 accept-encoding: gzip, deflate

6 connection: keep-alive


6 Apr 21:14:39 - e_request

6 Apr 21:14:39 - request GET 1.1 /favicon.ico

{"search":"","query":{},"pathname":"/favicon.ico","href":"/favicon.ico"}

0 host: localhost:3000
```

```
1 user-agent: Mozilla/5.0 (Macintosh; U; Intel Mac OS X 10_6_7; en-us)
AppleWebKit/533.20.25 (KHTML, like Gecko) Version/5.0.4 Safari/533.20.27

2 referer: http://localhost:3000/

3 cache-control: max-age=0

4 accept: */*

5 accept-language: en-us

6 accept-encoding: gzip, deflate

7 connection: keep-alive
```

You now have a tool for snooping on HTTP server events. This simple technique prints a detailed log of event data and the pattern can be used for any EventEmitter object. You can use this technique as a way to inspect the actual behavior of EventEmitter objects in your program.

Implementing a basic web server

This section presents the implementation of Basic Server, a basic web server. While Node includes an excellent HTTP Server object there are several additional protocol elements and services to wrap around that object to provide common website features.

Basic Server is, well, pretty basic. It demonstrates a way to implement some features including the following:

- Flexible request routing
- Automatically provide a parsed URL object
- Automatically extract the Host header (for virtual hosting)
- Automatically extract Cookie headers
- Satisfy favicon.ico requests
- Serving static files (HTML, JS, PNG, GIF, JPEG, and so on).
- Flexible server configuration

With these as the goals the following code comprises four Node modules, a CSS file, and one or more HTML files implementing Basic Server. Its small size is testament to Node's flexibility and power.

One item of preparation is to install the MIME module that's used to generate the correct Content-Type headers. We discuss the purpose of the module later if you're interested in what this is. In the meantime type this command:

```
$ npm install mime
```

The Basic Server implementation

Before we go into the code let's think a little about a general strategy to implement the goals we listed. Out of the box, Node provides this server architecture:

```
var server = http.createServer(function (req, res) {
   // handle the request
});
server.listen(port);
```

The goals we listed amount to implementing a HTTP request handler which inspects each request, and based on request attributes, to service each request with the appropriate functions. This architecture will separate the logic for inspecting and dispatching requests from the application business logic.

Basic Server core (basicserver.js)

The core of Basic Server is a module which creates an HTTP Server object, attaching to it the functions Basic Server uses to inspect requests, dispatching to appropriate functions.

Create a file named `basicserver.js` containing the following:

```
var http      = require('http');
var url       = require('url');

exports.createServer = function() {
  var htserver = http.createServer(function(req, res) {
    req.basicServer = {
      urlparsed: url.parse(req.url, true)
    };
    processHeaders(req, res);
    dispatchToContainer(htserver, req, res);
```

```
        });
        htserver.basicServer = { containers: [] };
        htserver.addContainer = function(host, path,
                                                module, options) {
          if (lookupContainer(
            htserver, host, path) !== undefined) {
            throw new Error("Already mapped "+host+"/"+path);
          }
          htserver.basicServer.containers.push({
            host: host, path: path,
            module: module, options: options });
          return this;
        }
        htserver.useFavIcon = function(host, path) {
          return this.addContainer(host, "/favicon.ico",
            require('./faviconHandler'),
            { iconPath: path });
        }
        htserver.docroot = function(host, path, rootPath) {
          return this.addContainer(host, path,
            require('./staticHandler'),
            { docroot: rootPath });
        }
        return htserver;
    }
```

What we have here, in the core of Basic Server, is a createServer function to create and return an HTTP Server object, while adding functionality to the server. The main show here is the request handler function. The strategy is to first add useful information to the request object (in the processHeaders function), and then dispatch to the appropriate handler (in the dispatchToContainer function). A second module is intended to be used with this to configure the server as desired for your application. We'll look at one such server configuration module shortly.

One tactic is to add useful data to both the server (htserver) and request (req) objects. JavaScript lets us do this as desired because of its loosely typed nature. All additions are made within an object, basicServer, that we attach to both htserver and req in this function. This way we can add any data to [htserver], and by hiding that data within the htserver.basicServer object, there is little chance of it interfering with other code.

The other thing we do here is add three functions to manage a list of containers. Containers roughly correspond to the Express router middleware we used in the previous chapter. The three functions add a container to the server (addContainer) and set up the two built-in containers, one to handle Favicon's (useFavIcon), the other to handle static files (docroot).

Containers are defined by four pieces of data as follows:

- A regular expression to match the Host header
- A regular expression to match the request URL
- An options object
- A handler function

Together this implements name-based virtual hosting, meaning Basic Server can answer requests for multiple domain names, by matching the Host header against container objects. We have more on this later.

The options object is meant to assist passing configuration data from the configuration module into the handler module, and the content of the options object is defined by the handler module.

For example with the Favicon handler, it contains the pathname for the image file to return for favicon requests. The path requested by the browser is always /favicon.ico, and this is the hard-coded path in the container.

There are several functions we used earlier but haven't looked at yet. The first of these, lookupContainer, looks in the containers array for a container matching the host and path in the HTTP request:

```
var lookupContainer = function(htserver, host, path) {
  for (var i = 0;
    i < htserver.basicServer.containers.length; i++) {
    var container = htserver.basicServer.containers[i];
    var hostMatches = host.toLowerCase().match(container.host);
    var pathMatches = path.match(container.path);
    if (hostMatches !== null && pathMatches !== null) {
      return {
        container: container,
          host: hostMatches,
          path: pathMatches };
    }
  }
  return undefined;
}
```

This is a fairly straightforward scan through an array using regular expressions to match the `host` and `path` against entries in the array. If one is found it's returned, otherwise we return `undefined`.

The next function, `processHeaders`, scans through the `req.headers` array looking for Cookie and Host headers, because both are useful for request dispatch. As you saw in the request handler discussed earlier, this function is called for every HTTP request:

```
var processHeaders = function(req, res) {
    req.basicServer.cookies = [];
    var keys = Object.keys(req.headers);
    for (var i = 0, l = keys.length; i < l; i++) {
        var hname = keys[i];
        var hval  = req.headers[hname];
        if (hname.toLowerCase() === "host") {
            req.basicServer.host = hval;
        }
        if (hname.toLowerCase() === "cookie") {
            req.basicServer.cookies.push(hval);
        }
    }
}
```

There are plenty of other HTTP headers (Accept, Accept-Encoding, Accept-Language, and User-Agent) which might be useful to save, depending on your application.

The last function, `dispatchToContainer`, does what its name implies. It looks up the matching container, dispatching the request to the container. Like `processHeaders` this function is called for every HTTP request:

```
var dispatchToContainer = function(htserver, req, res) {
  var container = lookupContainer(htserver,
    req.basicServer.host,
    req.basicServer.urlparsed.pathname);
  if (container !== undefined) {
    req.basicServer.hostMatches = container.host;
    req.basicServer.pathMatches = container.path;
    req.basicServer.container   = container.container;
    container.container.module.handle(req, res);
  } else {
    res.writeHead(404, { 'Content-Type': 'text/plain' });
    res.end("no handler found for "+
      req.host +"/"+ req.urlparsed.path);
  }
}
```

If no container is found the user gets an error page (status code 404) instead.

Handler modules export a function, handle, with the signature function(req,res). It is in dispatchToContainer where Basic Server dispatches requests by calling handle.

The Favicon handler (faviconHandler.js)

The Basic Server includes two built-in handler modules which we've not yet looked at. The first, faviconHandler.js, is the Favicon handler which is used to respond to Favicon requests. It is installed in Basic Server when your configuration module uses the useFavIcon function:

```
var fs = require('fs');
var mime = require('mime');
exports.handle = function(req, res) {
  if (req.method !== "GET") {
    res.writeHead(404, { 'Content-Type': 'text/plain' });
    res.end("invalid method " + req.method);
  } else if (req.basicServer.container.options.iconPath!== undefined) {
    fs.readFile(req.basicServer.container.options.iconPath,
    function(err, buf) {
      if (err) {
        res.writeHead(500, {
          'Content-Type': 'text/plain' });
        res.end(
          req.basicServer.container.options.iconPath
          +" not found");
      } else {
        res.writeHead(200, {
          'Content-Type':
          mime.lookup(req.basicServer.container.options.iconPath),
          'Content-Length': buf.length
        });
        res.end(buf);
      }
    });
  } else {
    res.writeHead(404, { 'Content-Type': 'text/plain' });
    res.end("no favicon");
  }
}
```

This handler is responsible for responding to requests for `favicon.ico`.

To reiterate, handler modules export a `function(req,res)` method named handle. Basic Server calls the `handle` function of the handler, listed in the container matching the incoming request. This one attempts to read in the file specified in `iconPath` sending it to the browser using the `res` object. Several error conditions are detected and error pages sent using `res`.

The MIME module is used to determine the correct MIME type based on the supplied icon file. Favicons can be any image type and we must inform the web browser of the image type being sent.

Since this handler is not valid for anything but GET requests, it checks the request method and responds with a 404 status code for anything but GET requests.

The static file handler (staticHandler.js)

Now let's look at the code required to respond to requests for files such as `.html` or `.css`. Create a file named `staticHandler.js` containing the following:

```
var fs   = require('fs');
var mime = require('mime');
var sys  = require('sys');
exports.handle = function(req, res) {
  if (req.method !== "GET") {
    res.writeHead(404, { 'Content-Type': 'text/plain' });
    res.end("invalid method " + req.method);
  } else {
    var fname = req.container.options.docroot +
      req.urlparsed.pathname;
    if (fname.match(/\/$/)) fname += "index.html";
    fs.stat(fname, function(err, stats) {
      if (err) {
        res.writeHead(500, {
          'Content-Type': 'text/plain' });
        res.end("file "+ fname +" not found " + err);
      } else {
        fs.readFile(fname, function(err, buf) {
          if (err) {
            res.writeHead(500, {
              'Content-Type': 'text/plain' });
            res.end("file "+
              fname +" not readable " + err);
          } else {
            res.writeHead(200, {
```

```
                    'Content-Type':
                    mime.lookup(fname),
                    'Content-Length': buf.length
                    });
                res.end(buf);
            }
        });
    }
    });
  }
}
```

This is the *staticHandler*, responsible for serving up files from the file system.

The `docroot` option is the pathname for a directory to hold the files it serves. It is a straightforward task to read in the specified file under the `docroot` directory, and send it to the browser using the `res` object—that is, if it exists—or otherwise no errors occur while reading the file.

One special case is the use of the MIME module (you can retrieve this from npm) to determine the correct `Content-Type` header. The MIME type is required so that the web browser can interpret the data correctly. We'll talk more about this later.

Another special case is if the requested URL ends in a /, then the handler changes the request by appending `index.html`.

A configuration for Basic Server (server.js)

Now that we have looked at all the components of Basic Server, we can look at building a working web server. Create a file named `server.js` with the following:

```
var port = 4080;
var server = require('./basicserver').createServer();
server.useFavIcon("localhost", "./docroot/favicon.png");
server.docroot("localhost", "/", "./docroot");
require('./httpsniffer').sniffOn(server);
server.listen(port);
```

This configuration specifies a directory named `docroot` to be the root directory for static files. In that directory, an image file named `favicon.png` is specified to be the Favicon. In other words, we've configured a simple web server with no dynamically generated pages.

The HTTP Sniffer is connected so that your console should show in excruciating detail every request your browser makes.

Before running the server let's look at the content to place into `docroot`.

It'll be helpful to add a few HTML files to have something to look at. They might look like this (which you can call `index.html`):

```
<html>
<head>
  <link href="/style.css" rel="stylesheet">
</head>
<body>
  <h1>Index</h1>
  <p><a href="page2.html">page 2</a></p>
  <p>
    Lorem ipsum dolor sit amet, consectetur adipiscing elit. Aliquam
    fringilla molestie leo eu tincidunt. Donec pulvinar porttitor
    dictum. Fusce at elit mauris, a ornare ipsum. Nulla congue nisi
    non ante pellentesque vel lobortis lacus varius. Nam metus ante,
    blandit in rutrum et, pellentesque eu velit. Nulla blandit
    placerat scelerisque. Morbi odio magna, accumsan sit amet
    pharetra eu, varius sit amet ipsum. Aenean interdum libero ut est
    hendrerit dictum. Suspendisse convallis pellentesque metus
    ac tempor. Nam  diam lectus, posuere eu rutrum id, facilisis vel
    tellus.
  </p>
</body>
```

You can create several similar HTML files using your favorite Lorem Ipsum generator (such as `http://www.lipsum.com/`) to supply the text. For convenience the HTML files can be linked together using `<a>` tags.

This HTML file references a CSS file named `style.css`, such as:

```
body {
  color: #00c;
  font-family: Verdana, Arial, Helvetica, sans-serif;
  background-color: #cf9
}
H1 {
  color: #ff6;
  background-color: #090;
  border: solid 5px #0f9
}
```

Finally, create a small image file named `favicon.png`. Favicons are the little image which web browsers show in the location bar. According to the Wikipedia page (`http://en.wikipedia.org/wiki/Favicon`) these can be a 32x32 or 48x48 image in nearly any image format, and display in every web browser except for Internet Explorer (which insists on `ICO` files).

Now run Basic Server:

```
$ node server.js
```

And in your web browser visit `http://localhost:4080`

Congratulations! You've now run the Basic Server. As configured your web browser will now show the content of the `index.html` you placed in the `docroot` directory:

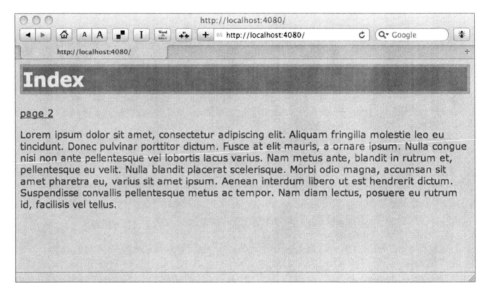

The Basic Server is very flexible with many things it can be made to do:

- Serve multiple virtual domains
- Add your own handlers
- Finish support for Cookie headers
- Implement authentication and HTTPS support

Virtual host configuration with Basic Server

Virtual hosting is a common need. If you need to support additional domain names you might do something like this to configure one directory per virtual domain:

```
// Two independent domains with separate content
bs.useFavIcon("example.com", "./example.com/favicon.png");
bs.docroot("example.com", "/", "./example.com");
bs.useFavIcon("example2.com", "./example2.com/favicon.png");
bs.docroot("example2.com", "/", "./example2.com");
// Parking one domain name on another
bs.useFavIcon("parked.com", "./example.com/favicon.png");
bs.docroot("parked.com", "/", "./example.com");
```

One can park a domain on top of another (configure it so two domains access the same container) by the example shown here. You can also use regular expressions like this:

```
bs.useFavIcon("parked.com|example.com",
  "./example.com/favicon.png");
bs.docroot("parked.com|example.com", "/", "./example.com");
```

A shorturl module for Basic Server

A common requirement is, instead of parking a domain on top of another, to cause requests on one domain to redirect to another. For example, redirecting www. example.com to just example.com (removing the www). Another example is services like tinyurl.com that provide a short URL which redirects to a long URL.

Both cases rely on sending a status code of either 301 (Moved Permanently) or 302 (Moved Temporarily) along with a Location header in the HTTP response. This combination signals the web browser to redirect over to another web location.

Let's implement a short handler module for Basic Server to send 302 redirects for a list of code values. Create a file named redirector.js:

```
var util = require('util');
var code2url = {
  'ex1': 'http://example1.com',
  'ex2': 'http://example2.com',
};
var notFound = function(req, res) {
  res.writeHead(404, { 'Content-Type': 'text/plain' });
  res.end("no matching redirect code found for "+
    req.basicServer.host +"/"+
    req.basicServer.urlparsed.pathname);
```

```
    }
    exports.handle = function(req, res) {
      if (req.basicServer.pathMatches[1]) {
        var code = req.basicServer.pathMatches[1];
        if (code2url[code]) {
          var url  = code2url[code];
          res.writeHead(302, { 'Location': url });
          res.end();
        } else {
          notFound(req, res);
        }
      } else {
        notFound(req, res);
      }
    }
```

This is a handler module for Basic Server. It expects a configuration line in `server.js` like this (before configuring the `docroot` container):

```
    server.addContainer(".*", "/l/(.*)$",  require('./redirector'), { });
```

We've used regular expressions for both the host and path portions of configuring the container. Any host name is matched because of the `.*` regular expression. The regular expression for matching the path name recognizes any path beginning with `/l/` and remembers the remainder as a submatch.

When you request `http://localhost:4080/l/code1`, the data about pathname matches appears in `req.basicServer.pathMatches`, with the submatch appearing in `req.basicServer.pathMatches[1]`. If everything matches up correctly, the handler returns an HTTP response with status code 302 and a Location header containing the URL retrieved from the `code2url` object.

MIME types and the MIME npm package

There are many details to get right in the HTTP protocol to implement a successful and correct web server. One of the details is the Content-Type header borrowed from the MIME protocol.

The MIME protocol was originally developed in the early 90s for improving e-mail capabilities; the HTTP protocol was developed in the same time frame, and both had the same core challenge. Namely, to identify the data format of the attachments to e-mail messages or HTTP requests. File extensions are insufficient to properly identify the file type because three characters (or so) are much too short to be a useful identifier, and there is no standard for file name extensions. Instead, we designed the Content-Type header and the whole MIME type standard as a generalized system of designating data types, and then made sure MIME types were useful for both e-mail and HTTP.

History lesson aside, it's mandatory to include the Content-Type header. The question is how does your application know what Content-Type to send? In some applications it's possible to know precisely what Content-Type headers to use because your application is sending specific known objects. This is especially true for smaller applications dealing with known data objects.

The staticHandler however, can be used to send any file and in the general case it won't know the correct Content-Type. It could be programmed with a list of common file extensions and matching Content-Type headers, but as was said earlier that's an insufficient solution. The best practice solution is to use an external configuration file, which is normally supplied by the operating system.

The MIME npm package uses the Apache projects `mime.types` file containing data on over 600 Content-Types. The mime module also supports adding your own MIME types should you need to support something specific.

Install the module:

```
$ npm install mime
```

Then in your code:

```
var mime = require('mime');
var mimeType = mime.lookup('image.gif'); // ==> image/gif
res.setHeader('Content-Type', mimeType);
```

Some related HTTP headers you might consider (`http://www.w3.org/Protocols/` and `http://en.wikipedia.org/wiki/List_of_HTTP_header_fields`) are as follows:

- **Content-Encoding**: Used when encoding the data such as gzip
- **Content-Language**: The language used in the content
- **Content-Length**: The number of bytes
- **Content-Location**: An alternate location to retrieve the data from
- **Content-MD5**: MD5 sum of the content body

Cookie handling

Another important feature is cookie support. The HTTP protocol is stateless, meaning that the web server doesn't know the identity of one requester from the identity of another requester. How then can we "log in" to a website if the protocol doesn't support any concept of state? The normal way is for a web server to send cookies to the browser, including cookies which identify the person who is logged in. Web browsers send cookies related to websites they're visiting on every request.

The Basic Server includes partial support for recognizing cookies sent by the browser. The request handler scans through the headers in the `req` object, identifying any Cookie headers, saving them into an array (`http://en.wikipedia.org/wiki/HTTP_Cookie`).

This retrieves cookies sent by the browser, with the remaining bit to parse `hval` to extract cookie values out of the string:

```
var keys = Object.keys(req.headers);
for (var i = 0, l = keys.length; i < l; i++) {
  var hname = keys[i];
  var hval = req.headers[hname];
  if (hname.toLowerCase() === "cookie") {
    req.basicServer.cookies.push(hval);
  }
}
```

To send a cookie, set a value for either Set-Cookie, or Set-Cookie2 header as follows:

```
res.setHeader('Set-Cookie2', .. cookie value ..);
```

Cookies are a structured text format, and cookie string parsing and formatting is an obvious candidate feature in a web framework like Basic Server (or Connect). There are a few existing libraries such as the following:

- `https://github.com/jed/cookies/`: Provides a somewhat complete cookie handling and validation layer, including support for signed cookies

- `https://github.com/bmeck/node-cookiejar`: Simple cookie parsing library

Virtual hosts and request routing

Virtual hosting is a method of hosting multiple domain names on the same IP address. As Basic Server shows, Node is capable of implementing name-based virtual hosting.

In name-based virtual hosting, the HTTP request will include a Host header specifying the domain name:

```
GET /path/to/request HTTP/1.1
Host: example.com
```

In Node the `req` object contains an array named `headers` which will contain the Host header. As Basic Server demonstrates, virtual hosting is easily implemented by inspecting the `headers` array and directing the request appropriately to the requested domain.

Making HTTP Client requests

Now that we've looked deeply at the HTTP server object, let's jump over to the other end of the wire. Node includes an HTTP Client object useful for making HTTP requests. It's enough to issue any kind of HTTP request, but for example it does not emulate a full browser so don't get delusions of this being a full scale test automation tool. With it you can build browser emulators or any other sort of HTTP client. For example, any REST web service can be called through an HTTP client object.

Let's start with some code inspired by the `wget` or `curl` commands to make HTTP requests and show the results. Create a file named `wget.js` containing this code:

```
var http = require('http');
var url  = require('url');
var util = require('util');

var argUrl = process.argv[2];
var parsedUrl = url.parse(argUrl, true);

var options = {
  host: null,
  port: -1,
  path: null,
  method: 'GET'
};
options.host = parsedUrl.hostname;
options.port = parsedUrl.port;
options.path = parsedUrl.pathname;
if (parsedUrl.search) options.path += "?"+parsedUrl.search;
```

```
var req = http.request(options, function(res) {
  util.log('STATUS: ' + res.statusCode);
  util.log('HEADERS: ' + util.inspect(res.headers));
  res.setEncoding('utf8');
  res.on('data', function (chunk) {
    util.log('BODY: ' + chunk);
  });
  res.on('error', function(err) {
    util.log('RESPONSE ERROR: ' + err);
  });
});
req.on('error', function(err) {
  util.log('REQUEST ERROR: ' + err);
});
req.end();
```

You can run the script as follows:

```
$ node wget.js http://example.com

11 Apr 21:34:35 - STATUS: 302

11 Apr 21:34:35 - HEADERS: {"location":"http://www.iana.org/domains/examp
le/","server":"BigIP","connection":"close","content-length":"0"}
```

This shows a HTTP response with status code 302 (redirect) telling your browser to instead go to http://www.iana.org/domains/example/, and indeed if you visit http://example.com in your browser it will redirect over to the iana.org page.

The purpose of wget.js is to make an HTTP request and show you voluminous detail of the response.

An HTTP request is initiated with the http.request method as follows:

```
var http = request('http');

var options = {
  host: 'example.com',
  port: 80,
  path: null,
  method: 'GET'
};
var request = http.request(options,
  function(response) { .. });
```

The `options` object describes the request to make, and the `callback` function is called when the response arrives. The `options` object is fairly straightforward with the `host`, `port`, and `path` fields specifying the URL being requested. The `method` field must be one of the HTTP verbs (GET, PUT, POST, and so on). You can also give a `headers` array for the headers in the HTTP request. For example, you might need to provide a cookie:

```
var options={

  headers: {
    'Cookie': '.. cookie value'
  }
};
```

The `response` object is itself an EventEmitter which emits `data` and `error` events. The `data` event is called as data arrives, and the `error` event is of course called on errors.

The `request` object is a WritableStream, which is useful for HTTP requests containing data, like PUT or POST. The data format in an HTTP request is specified by the MIME protocol. HTML forms will POST with a Content-Type of `multipart/form-data`, for example.

To send data over an HTTP ClientRequest simply call the `.write` function with properly formatted data. The data format is specified by the HTTP protocol with many options to handle a wide variety of uses. It's beyond the scope of this book to document the exact format of all variants of HTTP requests, so instead consider these libraries:

- `https://github.com/coolaj86/abstract-http-request`: Higher level wrapper around the HTTP request system
- `https://github.com/danwrong/restler`: A REST client library
- `https://github.com/maxpert/Reston`: A REST client library
- `https://github.com/pfleidi/node-wwwdude`: A REST client library
- `https://github.com/cloudhead/http-console`: A useful interactive shell for HTTP requests

Summary

We learned a lot in this chapter about the following:

- EventEmitters and their role in HTTP client and server objects
- Using an EventEmitter to separate acting on HTTP request data from the mechanics of receiving that data
- Listening to all the events of an HTTP object or other EventEmitter as a debugging aid
- Implementing an HTTP server
- Routing incoming requests in an HTTP server
- Using the MIME protocol to identify content data type
- Implementing an HTTP client

Now that we've learned the basics of implementing a web application with Node, we're ready to start towards useful applications. That means storing data somewhere, and acting on that data. In the next chapter, we'll look at several means of storing data and retrieving data from external datastores.

6
Data Storage and Retrieval

To round off this book we'll look at methods in Node for storing data. No matter how powerful Express is as a web framework, it can do little without storing data somewhere. The common best practice is to store data in some sort of database. Today the range of database technology serves a wide range of use cases, from traditional SQL data warehouses to modern NoSQL document-oriented databases, to simple key/value data stores, to web-service based query services like YQL.

In this chapter we'll implement two versions of a simple Notes application. The application demonstrates CRUD (Create, Read, Update, and Delete) basics using an Express based web application, and some SQL and MongoDB modules for Node.

Data storage engines for Node

Node does not include built-in support for any data storage system, other than reading and writing files in the file system. Using any other data storage system, such as databases, means you are using a module to interface with the database. The Node wiki lists a couple dozen modules interfacing with CouchDB, MongoDB, MySQL, Postgres, SQLite3, Memcache, REDIS, YQL, and others.

See: `https://github.com/joyent/node/wiki/modules#database`.

Generally you'll have to install both the module and its dependencies, including native code database client libraries. For example, the MySQL modules require a MySQL server and a MySQL client library to be available.

SQLite3—Lightweight in-process SQL engine

SQL databases don't necessarily require heavy-weight database servers with expensive database administrators. SQLite3 (`http://www.sqlite.org/`) is easy to set up: it's just a self-contained library linked into your application, and is a server-less, no-configuration-required SQL database engine. The node-sqlite3 project (`https://github.com/developmentseed/node-sqlite3`) interfaces sqlite3 into Node.

Installation

Installation is very simple if you have npm installed:

```
$ npm install sqlite3
```

Installing this module requires having the `sqlite3` library installed on your system, and the npm module which contains native code (in C) that links to the `sqlite3` library. The library is already installed on Mac OS X, and if not delivered with your favorite Linux distro it's just one package manager command away (for example, `apt-get install libsqlite3`). The `sqlite3` website (`http://sqlite.org/`) has documentation about using this database, its command-line tools, and C API.

Implementing the Notes application with SQLite3

To explore using `sqlite3` we'll implement a simple application to enter and display notes. The application will be used later using `MongoDB`.

Since it is an SQL database the Notes schema is described with SQL. The SQL `CREATE TABLE` command can be seen in `notesdb-sqlite3.js` in the next section:

```
CREATE TABLE IF NOT EXISTS notes (
    ts DATETIME,
    author VARCHAR(255),
    note TEXT
)
```

The field `ts` is a timestamp used to identify the note, `author` is meant to have the name of the author, and `note` contains the note.

Database abstraction module—notesdb-sqlite3.js

This is the database interface library to be used by the rest of this application, hiding the SQL commands within one module. It implements the four legs of CRUD with the functions add (to create), findNoteById (to read), edit (to update), and delete (to delete) Notes in the database.

The purpose of this module is encapsulating SQLite3 calls from the rest of the Notes application. It provides a few functions to set up the database table, add entries to the table, return all rows of the table, and delete entries from the table, which helps us take a step towards the model-view-controller architecture:

```javascript
var util    = require('util');
var sqlite3 = require('sqlite3');
sqlite3.verbose();
var db = undefined;
exports.connect = function(callback) {
  db = new sqlite3.Database("chap06.sqlite3",
    sqlite3.OPEN_READWRITE | sqlite3.OPEN_CREATE,
    function(err) {
      if (err) {
        utils.log('FAIL on creating database ' + err);
        callback(err);
      } else
        callback(null)
    }
  );
}
exports.disconnect = function(callback) {
  callback(null);
}
exports.setup = function(callback) {
  db.run("CREATE TABLE IF NOT EXISTS notes "+
    "(ts DATETIME, author VARCHAR(255), note TEXT)",
    function(err) {
      if (err) {
        util.log('FAIL on creating table ' + err);
        callback(error);
      } else
        callback(null);
    });
}
```

This is the administrative code, bringing in the modules, and functions for opening and closing the database, as well as setting up the database table. We have a hard-coded database name, so when the `connect` and `setup` functions are called a file, `chap06.sqlite`, will be created in the current directory.

This module shares the same API with a module named `notesdb-mongoose.js` we'll look at later in the chapter. That module will use Mongoose to talk with a MongoDB instance. For example, the `disconnect` function here is essentially empty, but the Mongoose version later actually disconnects from Mongoose:

```
exports.emptyNote = { "ts": "", author: "", note: "" };
exports.add = function(author, note, callback) {
  db.run("INSERT INTO notes ( ts, author, note) "+
    "VALUES ( ?, ? , ? );",
    [ new Date(), author, note ],
    function(error) {
      if (error) {
        util.log('FAIL to add ' + error);
        callback(error);
      } else
        callback(null);
    });
}
```

The `add` function adds an entry to the database, and is a straightforward use of SQL.

With SQLite3 the `.run` function takes a parameterized string where question marks indicate placeholders, and you must pass in values for the placeholders through an array as shown here. This approach with parameterized strings is common among SQL implementations in every programming language. With SQLite3 you are expected to provide one array element for every question mark in the SQL string. The SQL interface takes care of encoding the value correctly for the SQL statement.

The notable thing is that the caller provides a callback function, through which errors are indicated. The model does not know how to present the error to the user, and it's expected that the calling function will have a better idea of what to do about the error:

```
exports.delete = function(ts, callback) {
  db.run("DELETE FROM notes WHERE ts = ?;",
    [ ts ],
    function(err) {
      if (err) {
        util.log('FAIL to delete ' + err);
        callback(err);
```

```
        } else
          callback(null);
      });
  }
```

The `delete` function deletes notes from the database.

The notable thing here is that the timestamp is used to identify the note to delete, and all through this module we're doing the same to identify the note to operate on. The field `ts` in the database is initialized in the `add` function:

```
  exports.edit = function(ts, author, note, callback) {
    db.run("UPDATE notes "+
      "SET ts = ?, author = ?, note = ? "+
      "WHERE ts = ?",
      [ ts, author, note, ts ],
      function(err) {
        if (err) {
          util.log('FAIL on updating table ' + err);
          callback(err);
        } else
          callback(null);
      });
  }
```

The `edit` function supports updating a note with new values. We're using the UPDATE SQL statement along with parameters for the new values and the timestamp of the note to update:

```
  exports.allNotes = function(callback) {
    util.log(' in allNote');
    db.all("SELECT * FROM notes", callback);
  }
  exports.forAll = function(doEach, done) {
    db.each("SELECT * FROM notes", function(err, row) {
      if (err) {
        util.log('FAIL to retrieve row ' + err);
        done(err, null);
      } else {
        doEach(null, row);
      }
    }, done);
  }
```

The `allNotes` and `forAll` functions are two ways to operate on the entire set of Notes. In `allNotes` it collects all rows from the database into an array. In `forAll` there are two callback functions, `doEach` that is called for each row in the result set, and `done` that is called after the last row.

Clearly `allNotes` has potential for a bigger memory footprint than does `forAll`, which works with one row at a time:

```
exports.findNoteById = function(ts, callback) {
  var didOne = false;
  db.each("SELECT * FROM notes WHERE ts = ?",
    [ ts ],
  function(err, row) {
    if (err) {
      util.log('FAIL to retrieve row ' + err);
      callback(err, null);
    } else {
      if (!didOne) {
        callback(null, row);
        didOne = true;
      }
    }
  });
}
```

The `.findNoteById` function returns the data for one Note as identified by the timestamp. The timestamp should identify specific rows in the database, and we're also using a flag to ensure the callback is called only once, on the outside chance of additional database rows with the same timestamp.

Initializing the database—setup.js

The Node `sqlite3` module uses the `sqlite3` libraries to do its work, so of course all the normal `sqlite3` tools work with databases created using `node-sqlite3`. For example, a database can be created using the `sqlite3` command as follows:

```
Terminal — bash — 88×9
$ sqlite3 chap06.sqlite3
SQLite version 3.7.6
Enter ".help" for instructions
Enter SQL statements terminated with a ";"
sqlite> CREATE TABLE notes (ts DATETIME, author VARCHAR(255), note TEXT);
sqlite> .schema notes
CREATE TABLE notes (ts DATETIME, author VARCHAR(255), note TEXT);
sqlite> 
```

But you can also write a script, `setup.js`, to initialize a database this way using the `notesdb` module:

```
var util = require('util');
var async = require('async');
var notesdb = require('./notesdb-sqlite3');
// var notesdb = require('./notesdb-mongoose');
notesdb.connect(function(error) {
  if (error) throw error;
});
notesdb.setup(function(error) {
  if (error) {
    util.log('ERROR ' + error);
    throw error;
  }
  async.series([
    function(cb) {
      notesdb.add("Lorem Ipsum ",
        "Cras metus. Sed aliquet risus a tortor. Integer id quam.
        Morbi .. fermentum non, convallis id, sagittis at, neque.",
      function(error) {
        if (error) util.log('ERROR ' + error);
        cb(error);
      });
    }
  ],
    function(error, results) {
      if (error) util.log('ERROR ' + error);
      notesdb.disconnect(function(err) { });
    }
  );
});
```

The first notable item is having two require calls for different `notesdb` modules, where only `require('notesdb-sqlite3')` is actually being executed. We'll be reusing this same script later with the Mongoose module, and because their APIs are the same we can change only the module name to switch between databases.

This pre-populates the database and you can repeat `notesdb.add` as many times as you like. The consideration here is when is the correct time to call the `.disconnect` function. If we call `disconnect` before all the `add` operations are finished and some of them will fail. Remember that these functions run asynchronously and the `add` operations might randomly run out of the order of their appearance in the source code.

The `async` module is being used here to correctly orchestrate a series of `add` operations followed by `disconnect`. Normally callback functions run in the background and if the script were to run several `notesdb.add` calls followed by a `notesdb.disconnect`, the `disconnect` operation might run before all the `add` operations are finished. The `async` module is very useful. It can do many things, and the `async.series` function lets you execute one function after another, in order, and ensures the final function is executed after all the others are finished.

Display notes on the console—show.js

As we mentioned earlier, the `notesdb.forAll` function enables retrieving every note in the database. We can be use it to print the database to the console as follows:

```
var util = require('util');
var notesdb = require('./notesdb-sqlite3');
// var notesdb = require('./notesdb-mongoose');
notesdb.connect(function(error) {
  if (error) throw error;
});
notesdb.forAll(function(error, row) {
  util.log('ROW: ' + util.inspect(row));
}, function(error) {
  if (error) throw error;
  util.log('ALL DONE');
  notesdb.disconnect(function(err) { });
});
```

You can run the script as follows:

```
● ● ●                     Terminal — bash — 90×15
$ node show
6 Jul 15:39:32 - ROW: { ts: 1309991225472,
  author: 'Lorem Ipsum 12',
  note: 'Lorem ipsum dolor sit amet, consectetur adipiscing elit. Integer nec odio. Praese
nt libero. Sed cursus ante dapibus diam. Sed nisi. Nulla quis sem at nibh elementum imperd
iet. Duis sagittis ipsum. Praesent mauris. Fusce nec tellus sed augue semper porta. Mauris
  massa. Vestibulum lacinia arcu eget nulla. Class aptent taciti sociosqu ad litora torquen
t per conubia nostra, per inceptos himenaeos. Curabitur sodales ligula in libero. Sed dign
issim lacinia nunc.' }
6 Jul 15:39:32 - ROW: { ts: 1309991225490,
  author: 'Lorem Ipsum 23',
  note: 'Curabitur tortor. Pellentesque nibh. Aenean quam. In scelerisque sem at dolor. Ma
ecenas mattis. Sed convallis tristique sem. Proin ut ligula vel nunc egestas porttitor. Mo
rbi lectus risus, iaculis vel, suscipit quis, luctus non, massa. Fusce ac turpis quis ligu
la lacinia aliquet. Mauris ipsum. Nulla metus metus, ullamcorper vel, tincidunt sed, euism
```

Putting together the Notes web application—app.js

Now that we've seen how to make database calls through the `notesdb-sqlite3.js` module, let's put this together in a simple Express based web application, where `notesdb-sqlite3.js` serves as the model for the Notes application and `app.js` will serve as the controller. The view will be provided by some template files we'll see in a moment. Like the two scripts we've already looked at, `show.js` and `setup.js`, `app.js` is written to be easily switched between the `notesdb-sqlite3.js` and `notesdb-mongoose.js` modules:

```
var util    = require('util');
var url     = require('url');
var express = require('express');
var nmDbEngine = 'sqlite3';
// var nmDbEngine = 'mongoose';
var notesdb = require('./notesdb-'+nmDbEngine);
var app = express.createServer();
app.use(express.logger());
app.use(express.bodyParser());
app.register('.html', require('ejs'));
app.set('views', __dirname + '/views-'+nmDbEngine);
app.set('view engine', 'ejs');
```

Here is the administrative code to load in the required modules and set up the Express server components.

Here we need to highlight the `nmDbEngine` variable and its usages. This variable is used to name the database engine, to select the correct `notesdb` implementation, and to select the correct `views` directory. Both of these differ depending on database engine, while `app.js` can remain the same:

```
var parseUrlParams = function(req, res, next) {
  req.urlP = url.parse(req.url, true);
  next();
}
notesdb.connect(function(error) {
  if (error) throw error;
});
app.on('close', function(errno) {
  notesdb.disconnect(function(err) { });
});
```

Here we maintain the database connection using the `connect` and `disconnect` functions.

The `parseUrlParams` function is a route middleware function used in some of the router functions for parsing URL query parameters:

```
app.get('/', function(req, res) { res.redirect('/view'); });
app.get('/view', function(req, res) {
  notesdb.allNotes(function(err, notes) {
    if (err) {
      util.log('ERROR ' + err);
      throw err;
    } else
      res.render('viewnotes.html', {
        title: "Notes ("+nmDbEngine+")", notes: notes
      });
  });
});
```

Here we show the list of notes in the browser.

The first thing we do is redirect a request for / to /view by calling `res.redirect('/view')`. The /view page is being treated as the Notes application main interface, and many router functions redirect to this page.

Page rendering is done with the `viewnotes.html` template, which we'll look at a bit later. It is being sent two variables, `title` containing a page title string, and `notes` which is an array of notes. It handles rendering all the notes in the array it's given:

```
app.get('/add', function(req, res) {
  res.render('addedit.html', {
    title: "Notes ("+nmDbEngine+")",
      postpath: '/add',
      note: notesdb.emptyNote
  });
});
app.post('/add', function(req, res) {
  notesdb.add(req.body.author, req.body.note,
    function(error) {
      if (error) throw error;
      res.redirect('/view');
    });
});
```

Here we have the route functions to add notes to the database.

One implementation detail to discuss is the two router functions for /add. The function in `app.get('/add', ...)` is called when the user clicks on the **Add** button. Their browser will issue an HTTP GET request on /add. This function uses the `addedit.html` template to create a FORM, allowing the user to enter their note, and click the **Submit** button.

The `addedit.html` template is used for both /add and /edit operations, and it expects to be given a Note object. The `notesdb.emptyNote` object is, as its name implies, an empty Note suitable for use when there is no existing Note object.

The function in `app.post('/add', ...)` is called upon submitting the form, when the browser issues an HTTP POST request. Data entered by the user is sent in the request body, which is processed by the `bodyParser` (`app.use(express.bodyParser())`) middleware and is available in `req.body`. Hence we use the data entered by the user in the `req.body.author` and `req.body.note` variables:

```
app.get('/del', parseUrlParams, function(req, res) {
  notesdb.delete(req.urlP.query.id,
    function(error) {
      if (error) throw error;
      res.redirect('/view');
    });
});
```

This is the router function to delete Notes from the database.

We're using `parseUrlParams` as route middleware because the Note identifier will appear as a URL query parameter named id. Therefore, we can go ahead and write `req.urlP.query.id` to access the id parameter, rather than having to write the code to parse the URL. When the `notesdb.delete` operation is done we redirect back to the application home page at /view:

```
app.get('/edit', parseUrlParams, function(req, res) {
  notesdb.findNoteById(req.urlP.query.id,
    function(error, note) {
      if (error) throw error;
      res.render('addedit.html', {
        title: "Notes ("+nmDbEngine+")",
        postpath: '/edit',
        note: note
      });
    });
});
app.post('/edit', function(req, res) {
  notesdb.edit(req.body.id, req.body.author, req.body.note,
```

```
        function(error) {
          if (error) throw error;
          res.redirect('/view');
        });
      });
    app.listen(3000);
```

Here we have the router functions to edit Notes in the database.

We're again using `parseUrlParams` to get the Note `id` from URL query parameters, using it to retrieve the Note using the `notesdb.findNoteById` function. You'll notice that we're again rendering the page using `addedit.html` but this time are sending it the Note retrieved from the database.

The `postpath` variable was earlier set to `/add` and this time is set to `/edit`. This variable is the destination for the form in `addedit.html` ensuring the correct `app.post` function is called, either `app.post('/add',..)` or `app.post('/edit',..)`.

Notes application templates

Before we can run the Notes application we must set up the templates referenced in `app.js`, which is `viewnotes.html`, `addedit.html` and `layout.html`.

The following files must be placed in a directory named `views-sqlite3`. Later we will create another directory, `views-mongoose`, to hold the Mongoose templates.

Let's start with `layout.html`:

```html
<html>
  <head><title><%= title %></title></head>
  <body>
    <h1><%= title %></h1>
    <p><a href='/view'>View</a> | <a href='/add'>Add</a></p>
    <%- body %>
  </body>
<html>
```

This is the Notes application page layout, which is pretty straightforward. It handles the `title` variable sent in the `res.render` calls in `app.js`.

Now let's look at `viewnotes.html`:

```html
<table><% notes.forEach(function(note) { %>
  <tr><td>
    <p><%= new Date(note.ts).toString() %>:
      by <b><%= note.author %></b></p>
    <p><%= note.note %></p>
  </td><td>
```

```
    <form method='GET' action='/del'>
      <input type='submit' value='Delete' />
      <input type='hidden' name='id' value='<%=
        note.ts %>'>
    </form>
    <br/><form method='GET' action='/edit'>
      <input type='submit' value='Edit' />
      <input type='hidden' name='id' value='<%=
        note.ts %>'>
    </form>
  </td></tr><% }); %></table>
```

This version is for the SQLite3 Notes application. It shows the timestamp, title, and content of the Note, as well as two forms allowing the user to either delete (/del) or edit (/edit) the Note.

There's a hidden form value, id, and for the SQLite3 Notes application we're using the timestamp to identify Notes. Earlier while discussing the app.post functions for delete (/del) or edit (/edit) operations we parsed the URL parameters to get the id param, which comes from this hidden form value.

Now let's look at addedit.html:

```
  <form method='POST' action='<%= postpath %>'>
    <% if (note) { %>
      <input type='hidden' name='id' value='<%= note.ts %>'>
    <% } %>
      <input type='text' name='author' value='<%= note.author %>'/>
      <br/>
      <textarea rows=5 cols=40 name='note' ><%=
        note.note
      %></textarea>
      <br/><input type='submit' value='Submit' />
  </form>
```

This form is used for both adding (/add) and editing (/edit) Notes. The postpath variable gets set to the form destination URL. Other form values come from the Note object passed from app.js, which might be the emptyNote object.

Running the SQLite3 Notes application

Now that we have all the pieces together, the Notes application can be run. If you ran the `setup.js` script earlier, the database has already been set up, otherwise do so now. You can now run it by using the following:

```
$ node app
```

Because of the `app.listen(3000)` statement you can visit the application at `http://localhost:3000/`. It will look something like the following:

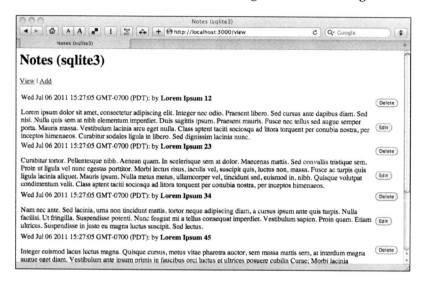

If you click on a **Delete** button the browser simply refreshes, but you'll notice one item is missing, the one you clicked on. The immediate refresh is because the `app.get('/del'..)` implementation just calls `notesdb.delete`, immediately redirecting back to `/view`.

The next thing you can do is either add (clicking the **Add** link) or edit (clicking an **Edit** button) a Note. The screen looks like the following :

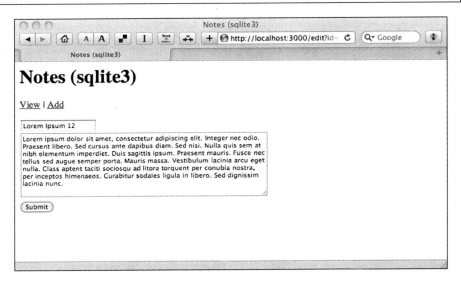

Clicking the **Submit** button calls either `app.post('/add',..)` or `app.post('/edit',..)`, both of which update the database and redirect the browser to the `/view` page.

Handling and debugging errors

If you make a coding mistake or when other issues arise, error objects will be thrown inside the application. Debugging the application means displaying the errors to know when and where they occur. In the Notes application we used `util.log` statements to display errors as they happened. Inside the `notesdb-sqlite3.js` module we use callbacks to send error objects back to `app.js`, which then throws the error.

One of the defaults built into Express displays this nice developer-friendly stack trace in the browser:

The function `app.error` is provided by Express to capture exceptions thrown by a `route` function, or executed with a `next(error)` call.

It's easy to insert an error if you want to explore this behavior, such as this contrived call of a method on a null object:

```
app.get('/del', parseUrlParams, function(req, res) {
  var notAllowed = null;
  notAllowed.delete();
  ..
});
```

The error page we just showed, while effective for a developer, isn't very user friendly, is it? Let's try to make it better.

One option is to insert this into `app.js`:

```
app.use(express.errorHandler({ dumpExceptions: true }));
```

The browser window will show a simple message "**Internal Server Error**". It is less user unfriendly, but still not very nice. The developer-friendly stack trace does get printed to `stderr` where it won't bother the user with unnecessary details, while still being available to you, the developer.

The starting point to a proper user-friendly error page is an `app.error` function like the following:

```
app.error(function(err, req, res) {
  res.render('500.html', {
    title: "Notes ("+nmDbEngine+") ERROR", error: err
  });
});
```

There are plenty of options in implementing this function, such as generating a different error page based on the kind of error object it receives, or maybe showing a picture of birds lifting a whale out of the ocean. The specifics are up to you, and for demonstration purposes let's just use this error page template, `500.html`:

```
<b>Internal Server Error</b>
ERROR: <%= error %>
```

With this much in place we get this error displayed in the browser:

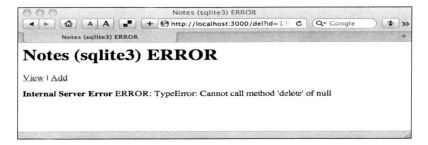

Using other SQL databases with Node

SQLite3 is by no means the be all and end all of SQL databases. We chose it for the Notes application due to the easy setup and configuration. You should consider SQLite3 whenever your database needs can live on a single computer. The other SQL databases have other compelling features such as supporting distributed database access, high transactional throughput, mirroring, and more.

Low level (close to the SQL):

- Node-mysql (`https://github.com/felixge/node-mysql`) is a pure Node JavaScript implementation of the MySQL client protocol.

- Node-mysql-native (`https://github.com/sidorares/nodejs-mysql-native`) wraps the native MySQL client library as a Node module.

- Node-mysql-libmysqlclient (`https://github.com/Sannis/node-mysql-libmysqlclient`) are MySQL bindings for Node using libmysqlclient.

- Node-postgres (`https://github.com/brianc/node-postgres`) is a heavily tested Node client for connecting to Postgres. It has both, pure JavaScript and native bindings.

- Node-sqlite3 (`https://github.com/developmentseed/node-sqlite3`) is an asynchronous non-blocking SQLite3 bindings for Node.

- Node-DBI (`https://github.com/DrBenton/Node-DBI`) is an SQL database abstraction layer.

Higher level (has ORM features):

- FastLegS (`https://github.com/didit-tech/FastLegS`) PostgreSQL ORM built on top of node-postgres

- Node-orm (`https://github.com/dresende/node-orm`) Node Object-Relational-Mapping meant to be for multiple databases

- persistence.js (`https://github.com/zefhemel/persistencejs`) is an asynchronous JavaScript object-relational mapping library which can be used in both browser and Node server applications

- Sequelize (`https://github.com/sdepold/sequelize`) is an object-relational mapper for Node and MySQL

Mongoose—Node interface to MongoDB

MongoDB is one of the leading "nosql" databases (where nosql of course means "no SQL"). They describe it as a "scalable, high performance, open source, document-oriented database". It uses JSON-style documents with no predefined rigid schema, and a large number of advanced features. You can see their website for more information and documentation: `http://www.mongodb.org/`.

Mongoose is one of several modules for accessing MongoDB. It is an object modeling tool, meaning that your program defines Schema objects describing its data, and Mongoose takes care of storage in MongoDB. It's a very powerful object modeling tool for Node and MongoDB, with embedded documents, a flexible typing system for fields, field validation, virtual fields, and more. See: `http://mongoosejs.com/`.

Installing Mongoose

Installation is very simple if you have npm installed:

```
$ npm install mongoose
```

Before using Mongoose you must have a MongoDB instance running. There are prebuilt binary packages on `mongodb.com` or it's available through package systems on most Linux distributions. On Mac OS X it is available through MacPorts. You can consult their website for more information, especially their Quickstart guide for your operating system (`http://www.mongodb.org/display/DOCS/Quickstart`).

There's a two-step procedure to verify that you can use MongoDB. The first part is to start the MongoDB server (`mongod`) with a local data directory, as shown in the following screenshot:

```
  ●  ○  ○              Terminal — mongod — 90×11
$
$ rm -rf data
$ mkdir data
$ mongod --dbpath ./data
Thu Jul  7 15:19:22 MongoDB starting : pid=18682 port=27017 dbpath=./data 64-bit
Thu Jul  7 15:19:22 db version v1.6.6-pre-, pdfile version 4.5
Thu Jul  7 15:19:22 git version: nogitversion
Thu Jul  7 15:19:22 sys info: Darwin tippy.local 10.7.0 Darwin Kernel Version 10.7.0: Sat
Jan 29 15:17:16 PST 2011; root:xnu-1504.9.37~1/RELEASE_I386 i386 BOOST_LIB_VERSION=1_45
Thu Jul  7 15:19:22 [initandlisten] waiting for connections on port 27017
Thu Jul  7 15:19:22 [websvr] web admin interface listening on port 28017
```

This is useful for development use, which we'll be doing in a moment. You can kill the process with *Control-C* any time you like, and start over with a fresh clean data directory by running the commands shown here.

The next step to verify you can use MongoDB is to run the user interaction in their quickstart guide (see the previous link):

```
  ●  ○  ○              Terminal — mongo — 72×8
$ mongo
MongoDB shell version: 1.6.6-pre-
connecting to: test
> db.foo.save( { a : 1 } )
> db.foo.find()
{ "_id" : ObjectId("4e16313464a1126e2a76a030"), "a" : 1 }
>
```

This inserts a document (the JSON { a: 1 }) into the collection named foo. The command db.foo.find is used to query the collection foo and, because there's no query parameters, it lists all elements in the collection, which are then printed in JSON notation. The MongoDB website has full documentation on using this database, including the Mongo shell.

Implementing the Notes application with Mongoose

To explore using Mongoose we'll implement another version of the Notes application.

The schema we'll be using is similar to the SQL version of the schema, but written using the Mongoose object notation:

```
var NoteSchema = new Schema({
    ts      : { type: Date, default: Date.now },
    author : String,
```

```
  note    : String
});
mongoose.model('Note', NoteSchema);
```

The fields used have the same purpose as in the SQL schema. The data types are JavaScript objects because that's what Mongoose uses. The `ts` field uses a default value in case a `ts` value is not provided when creating the object.

Let's get on with the code.

Database abstraction module—notesdb-mongoose.js

As with the `sqlite3` Notes application, this is the database interface library to be used by the rest of this application. It implements the three legs of CRUD with the functions `add` (to create), `findNoteById` (to read), `edit` (to update), and `delete` (to delete) Note documents in the database.

As with the `sqlite3` Notes application, `notesdb-mongoose.js` implements the model aspect of the model-view-controller architecture:

```
var util = require('util');
var mongoose = require('mongoose');
var Schema = mongoose.Schema;
var dburl = 'mongodb://localhost/chap06';
exports.connect = function(callback) {
  mongoose.connect(dburl);
}
exports.disconnect = function(callback) {
  mongoose.disconnect(callback);
}
```

This is the administrative code, bringing in the modules as well as the `.connect` and `.disconnect` functions. The `dburl` variable is used to connect with the running MongoDB. These handle connecting with MongoDB, and the programs are expected to call `.connect` when they start and `.disconnect` before they stop:

```
exports.setup = function(callback) { callback(null); }
var NoteSchema = new Schema({
  ts      : { type: Date, default: Date.now },
  author : String,
  note    : String
});
mongoose.model('Note', NoteSchema);
var Note = mongoose.model('Note');
exports.emptyNote = { "_id": "", author: "", note: "" };
```

This part defines the schema, but then we have already discussed it. The schema is created by `var NoteSchema = new Schema(...)`. It is then registered as a Mongoose model with this code:

```
mongoose.model('Note', NoteSchema);
var Note = mongoose.model('Note');
```

With a schema and model registered, your program can proceed with creating documents in the database:

```
exports.add = function(author, note, callback) {
    var newNote = new Note();
    newNote.author = author;
    newNote.note   = note;
    newNote.save(function(err) {
      if (err) {
        util.log('FATAL '+ err);
        callback(err);
      } else
        callback(null);
    });
}
```

With Mongoose you do this by creating a new instance of the object, assigning data to its fields, and calling the `.save` method. In this case, we are not providing a value for the `ts` field, but the schema definition declares a default value:

```
exports.delete = function(id, callback) {
exports.findNoteById(id, function(err, doc) {
    if (err)
      callback(err);
    else {
      util.log(util.inspect(doc));
      doc.remove();
      callback(null);
    }
  });
}
```

Deleting a Note from the database is a two step process. You have to first retrieve the Note from the database by using a function, `findNoteById`, that we'll see in a minute, and then call that object's `.remove` method:

```
exports.edit = function(id, author, note, callback) {
    exports.findNoteById(id, function(err, doc) {
      if (err)
```

```
        callback(err);
      else {
        doc.ts     = new Date();
        doc.author = author;
        doc.note   = note;
        doc.save(function(err) {
          if (err) {
            util.log('FATAL '+ err);
            callback(err);
          } else
            callback(null);
        });
      }
    });
}
```

Likewise, updating a Note is also a two step process. You first retrieve the Note, assign new values to its fields, and then call the object's .save method:

```
exports.allNotes = function(callback) {
  Note.find({}, callback);
}
exports.forAll = function(doEach, done) {
  Note.find({}, function(err, docs) {
    if (err) {
      util.log('FATAL '+ err);
      done(err, null);
    }
    docs.forEach(function(doc) {
      doEach(null, doc);
    });
    done(null);
  });
}
var findNoteById = exports.findNoteById = function(id,
  callback) {
  Note.findOne({ _id: id }, function(err, doc) {
    if (err) {
      util.log('FATAL '+ err);
      callback(err, null);
    }
    callback(null, doc);
  });
}
```

Now we see the three functions to retrieve Notes from the database.

In the `allNotes` and `forAll` functions we use the `Notes.find` method. This and the Query object used behind the scenes, are a powerful part of Mongoose. It's analogous to the `WHERE` clauses in SQL `SELECT` statements but is cleaner and easier to read. In both these functions the Query object is empty, which causes Mongoose to retrieve every document in the Notes collection.

In the `.findNoteById` function we call `Note.findOne` to find a specific Note identified by its `_id` field. We do this by passing in a Query object, `{ _id: id }`, to match the `id` against the `_id` field. MongoDB provides a guaranteed-to-be-unique ID for every document it stores, the `_id` field. It can serve the same purpose we had for the `ts` field in the `sqlite3` Notes application, so of course we use the `_id` field value to identify Notes. The Mongoose Query object can do much more than this, which you can learn about on `mongoosejs.org`.

Initializing the database—setup.js

As with SQLite3, there are two ways to initialize the database. You can use the mongo shell commands as shown in the following screenshot:

```
$
$ mongo
MongoDB shell version: 1.6.6-pre-
connecting to: test
> use chap06;
switched to db chap06
> db.notes.save({ ts: "Tue May 10 2011 20:26:38 GMT-0700 (PDT)", author: "so
meone", note: "A meaningful note" });
> db.notes.find();
{ "_id" : ObjectId("4e16484f64f7b4392f563b7a"), "ts" : "Tue May 10 2011 20:2
6:38 GMT-0700 (PDT)", "author" : "someone", "note" : "A meaningful note" }
>
```

The other way is with the `setup.js` script that we used earlier. It contains a pair of lines to select between `notesdb-sqlite3` and `notesdb-mongoose`.

```
// var notesdb = require('./notesdb-sqlite3');
var notesdb = require('./notesdb-mongoose');
```

Make the change shown here to swap which line is commented out, then run the script this way:

```
$ node setup
```

Nothing is printed, but you can use `show.js` to display the database and see what's there.

Display notes on the console—show.js

Displaying every item from the database is also done with the `show.js` script we used earlier. Simply make the same change we did in `setup.js`, and run the script as follows:

```
$ node show
7 Jul 17:20:58 - ROW: { doc:
  { ts: Fri, 08 Jul 2011 00:13:22 GMT,
    _id: 4e164ba289dc189149000001,
    note: 'Lorem ipsum dolor sit amet, consectetur adipiscing elit.
        Integer nec odio. Praesent .. Sed dignissim lacinia nunc.',
   author: 'Lorem Ipsum 12' },
  activePaths:
  { paths:
    { note: 'init',
      author: 'init',
      _id: 'init',
      ts: 'init' },
    states: { init: [Object], modify: {}, require: {} },
    stateNames: [ 'require', 'modify', 'init' ] },
  saveError: null,
  isNew: false,
  pres: { save: { serial: [Object], parallel: [] } },
  errors: undefined }
```

Putting it together in an application—app.js

Since `notesdb-mongoose.js` has the same API as `notesdb-sqlite.js`, we have been able to reuse `setup.js` and `show.js` with minimal modification. The same is true with `app.js`. The modification is slightly different but with the same intent. However, we must use different template files because of certain differences.

In `app.js` make the following change:

```
// var nmDbEngine = 'sqlite3';
var nmDbEngine = 'mongoose';
```

Now, make a directory named `views-mongoose` and prepare to create the following template files:

1. The first, `layout.html`, is the same as before so let's make a copy:

    ```
    $ cp views-sqlite3/layout.html views-mongoose/layout.html
    ```

2. The next, `viewnotes.html`, is identical to the previous one, except you change the hidden `id` input tag to read as follows:

    ```
    <input type='hidden' name='id' value='<%= note._id %>'>
    ```

3. Similarly, duplicate `addedit.html`, and edit the hidden `id` input tag to read as follows:

    ```
    <input type='hidden' name='id' value='<%= note._id %>'>
    ```

The difference between these templates and the SQLite3 version is the value of the hidden `id` form field. Like we noted earlier, Mongo provides an `_id` value in every document it stores, serving as a globally unique identifier.

Now we have all the pieces together to run the Mongoose Notes application:

```
$ node app
```

You can go ahead and visit `http://localhost:3000/` in your browser, as we did here. It looks almost precisely the same as the SQLite3 version of the application, but with a different title as shown in the following screenshot:

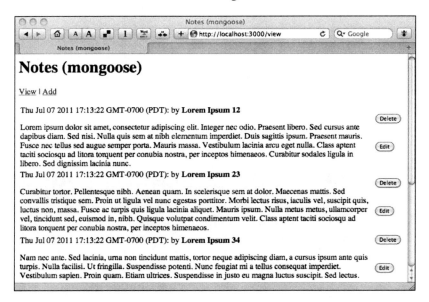

This version of the Notes application behaves exactly the same and both versions of the Notes application are a demonstration of using SQL and Mongo based datastores.

Other MongoDB database support

Mongoose isn't the only game in town when it comes to using MongoDB with Node.

One thing you'll find surprising is the difference between the MongoDB shell and the Node MongoDB module APIs. Since the MongoDB shell uses a JavaScript command interpreter, you might think they'd have the same API. Despite the many modules which claim similarity to the MongoDB shell, none of them use the same API:

- Node-mongodb (`https://github.com/orlandov/node-mongodb`) is an experimental asynchronous Node interface to MongoDB
- node-mongodb-native (`https://github.com/christkv/node-mongodb-native`) is another driver
- node-mongolian (`https://github.com/marcello3d/node-mongolian`) is an "awesome" driver that "attempts to closely approximate the MongoDB shell"
- Mongolia (`https://github.com/masylum/mongolia`) is a flexible "non-magical" layer above MongoDB, but is not an ORM
- Mongoose (`http://www.learnboost.com/mongoose/`) which we just used, is an ORM built on top of MongoDB
- Mongous (`https://github.com/amark/mongous`) is a "dead simple" interface to MongoDB with a jQuery-like syntax
- node-nosql-thin (`https://github.com/dmcquay/node-nosql-thin`) is a "thin" interface library to MongoDB that may later support other "NoSQL databases"

A quick look at authenticating your users

There are many application types where users log in to use privileged features. Since HTTP is a stateless protocol the only way to authenticate a user is by sending a cookie to their browser, after making them perform some action to verify their identity. The cookie would contain that data the application can use to verify the user. We're going to take a quick tour through implementing a login form, sending a cookie to the browser, and preventing access to Notes unless the cookie is present.

We start with a couple of modifications to `app.js`, the first of which is the server object configuration to add the `cookieParser` middleware:

```
var app = express.createServer();
app.use(express.logger());
app.use(express.cookieParser());
app.use(express.bodyParser());
```

The next step is to add a small route middleware function to check whether the user is allowed to have access. In this case we will only check if the cookie is equal to AOK, because that's the universal signal that everything is alright:

```
var checkAccess = function(req, res, next) {
  if (!req.cookies
    || !req.cookies.notesaccess
    || req.cookies.notesaccess !== "AOK") {
      res.redirect('/login');
  } else {
    next();
  }
}
```

The `cookieParser` middleware does a lot of heavy lifting here looking for cookies, parsing them, and putting their values in the `req` object. When a cookie is present it's value appears in `req.cookies`, such that we can access its value like we do here. If there are no cookies, or there is no `notesaccess` cookie, or if its value is not AOK, then the browser is redirected to the `/login` URL.

Before we look at the `/login` URL handler, let's add the `cookieParser` middleware to the Notes application routes. It's very simple:

```
app.get('/view', checkAccess, function(req, res) {
 ..
});
```

Specifically we add a call to `checkAccess` in the definition for every router function. This ensures that `checkAccess` is called for every URL in Notes and that every Notes URL is protected. Any URLs which aren't to be protected must not use the `checkAccess` route middleware function.

These two router functions handle the `/login` URL:

```
app.get('/login', function(req, res) {
  res.render('login.html', {
    title: "Notes LOGIN ("+nmDbEngine+")",
  });
});
```

```
app.post('/login', function(req, res) {
  // TBD check credentials entered in form
  res.cookie('notesaccess', 'AOK');
  res.redirect('/view');
});
```

And then finally this uses the following template, `login.html`:

```
<form method='POST' action='/login'>
  <p>Click the <i>Login</i> to log in.</p>
  <input type='submit' value='Login' />
</form>
```

There are a few bits to fill in here if you were to implement a real security system.

When the user's browser is redirected to /login by the checkAccess function, the first router function renders the login.html template in the browser, which looks like the following screenshot:

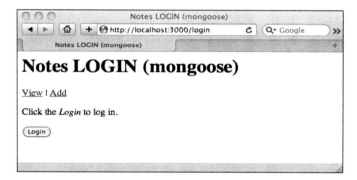

A real security system would have fields for at least a username and password. Instead we'll skip this and just ask the user to click the **Login** button.

The button is in a Form, which causes the app.post('/login'..) route function to be called. That function, if this were a real security system, would check the user credentials supplied in the login form, and only issue the authentication cookie if they match a user in the user database. Instead the route function issues the AOK cookie value and redirects the browser back to the /view URL.

While this left out several parts to a real security system, it contains the bones of such a system. There are many websites which have a user login form, which use and check authentication cookies on every page request. We have implemented functions to check for an authentication cookie and correct cookie value, a redirect to a login form, a check of the login form, and then send an authentication cookie to the browser.

Summary

We learned a lot in this chapter about data storage in Node. It's of course a key feature to many kinds of applications, so let's review what we learned:

- Node doesn't include built-in support for data storage engines, but the Node community has developed modules interfacing with more data storage engines than you knew existed

- Installing a data storage engine module probably means installing dependencies such as servers and client libraries

- SQLite3 is a no setup, no configuration required way to develop SQL applications

- A nearly identical web application can drive either SQL or MongoDB data storage

- ORM techniques are probably best used atop SQL data storage, but the community has developed ORMs for MongoDB and CouchDB anyway

- How to implement the model-view-controller architecture (partially)

- Handling form submission in an Express application

- Document-oriented database systems like MongoDB are closer to modern programming languages and applications than is SQL

We've come a long way in this book. We started with an overview of Node and the sort of software it can be used to implement. Then we learned how to install Node and npm for both development and deployment scenarios, and with those basics out of the way we developed Node modules and several applications to learn about building web applications, HTTP client and server applications, the Node event loop, converting long-running CPU intensive algorithms into ones that work with the Node event loop, distributing work to background processes using web services, and bringing data from a database into a Node application.

Index

Symbols

.use method 80

A

absolute module identifiers 39
addedit.html template 131, 133
add function 123, 124
adduser command 56
algorithmic refactoring 74
allNotes function 126
app-connect.js 81
app.js 129, 131
application
  external dependencies, bundling with 41-43
app-node.js 65, 72
apt-get tool 45
asynchronous event-driven architecture
  about 10
  versus threads 11, 12

B

Basic Server core 104-106
basicserver.js file 104
basic web server
  about 103
  capabilities 112
  configuring 110, 112
  cookie handling 116
  favicon handler 108, 109
  implementing 104
  shorturl module 113, 114
  static file handler 109, 110
  virtual host configuration 113
  virtual hosting 117

bin tag 46
blocking I/O 10

C

Cluster 34
command-line tools, Node
  node 24
  node-waf 24
CommonJS module system 10, 38, 59
complex modules 44, 45
config set command 57
configuration, basic web server 110, 112
configuration settings, npm 56, 57
Connect
  about 9, 64, 77
  connecting with 79, 81
  installing 78
  Math Wizard, implementing with 78
  server object, setting up 79
Connect based Node application
  running 79
connect function 129
containers 106
Content-Type header 115
cookie handling 116
cookies 116
CouchDB 121
count variable 38
CPAN 45
CPU cores
  using, on multi-core systems 33, 35
Create, Read, Update, and Delete. *See*
    CRUD
createServer function 105
CREATE TABLE command 122

CRUD 121
curl command 117

D

database
  initializing 126, 127
  notes, adding to 131
  notes, deleting from 131
  notes, editing in 132
  printing, to console 128
database abstraction module, Sqlite3 123-126
database connection
  maintaining 129
data storage engines 121
db.foo.find command 139
Debian's launchtool 30
delete function 123, 125
developer tools
  about 19
  installing, in home directory 19-21
  installing, in system-wide directory 21
  installing on Linux, from package management systems 23
  installing on Mac OS X, with homebrew 22
  installing on Mac OS X, with MacPorts 22
developer tools installation, on Mac OS X
  about 19
  home directory, installing in 19-21
  installing, on Linux from package management systems 23
  multiple Node installs, maintaining simultaneously 23, 24
  system-wide directory, installing in 21
  with homebrew 22
  with MacPorts 22
development environment, Node
  system requisites 17, 18
directories tag 47
disconnect function 124, 129
dispatch function 77
dispatchToContainer function 105-108
docroot option 110
doEach function 126
done function 126

E

edit function 123, 125
encapsulation
  example 38
errors
  handling, in Express Math Wizard 88
EventEmitter class 98
EventEmitter object
  about 98
  events 99, 100
  events, receiving with 98, 99
  events, sending with 98, 99
event names 99
events
  about 99
  receiving, with EventEmitter object 98, 99
  sending, with EventEmitter object 98, 99
explore command 53
Express 121
  about 64
  Math Wizard, implementing with 81
Express Math Wizard
  data services 88
  errors, handling 88
  implementing 82-87
  mathematics server 89-92
  parameterized URLs 89
express module 42
external dependencies
  bundling, with application 41-43

F

factorial-node.js 69
FastLegS 138
Favicon 80, 102
Favicon handler 108, 109
faviconHandler.js file 108
fibonacci numbers 70
fibo-node.js 70
filters 78
findNoteById function 123, 126
forAll function 126
forever 30
forms module 43

run function 124

S

Semantic Versioning model 57
Sequelize 138
set command 56
setup.js 126, 127, 143
shorturl module 113, 114
show.js 128
sniffOn function 101
SQLite3
  about 121, 122
  app.js 129, 131
  database abstraction module 123-126
  database, initializing 126, 127
  errors, debugging 135, 136
  errors, handling 135, 136
  installing 122
  Notes application, implementing with 122
  Notes application templates 132, 133
  notes, displaying on console 128
sqlite3 Notes application
  running 134, 135
square-node.js 69
start method 98
static file handler 109, 110
staticHandler.js file 109
static middleware 80
Swing 8
system requisites, Node
  about 17
  POSIX-like operating systems 17
system-wide modules 43, 44

T

tar-gzip tarballs 46
threads
  versus asynchronous event-driven architec-
    ture 11, 12
top-level module identifiers 39

U

Ubuntu's Upstart tool 30
unpublish command 56
UPDATE SQL statement 125

URL query parameters
  handling 66, 67
user authentication 146-148

V

V8 engine 8
view command 49
viewnotes.html template 130
virtual host configuration, basic web server
    113
virtual hosting 117

W

Web frameworks 64
wget command 117

Y

YQL 121
YSlow 73
yum tool 45

Thank you for buying
Node Web Development

About Packt Publishing

Packt, pronounced 'packed', published its first book "*Mastering phpMyAdmin for Effective MySQL Management*" in April 2004 and subsequently continued to specialize in publishing highly focused books on specific technologies and solutions.

Our books and publications share the experiences of your fellow IT professionals in adapting and customizing today's systems, applications, and frameworks. Our solution based books give you the knowledge and power to customize the software and technologies you're using to get the job done. Packt books are more specific and less general than the IT books you have seen in the past. Our unique business model allows us to bring you more focused information, giving you more of what you need to know, and less of what you don't.

Packt is a modern, yet unique publishing company, which focuses on producing quality, cutting-edge books for communities of developers, administrators, and newbies alike. For more information, please visit our website: www.packtpub.com.

About Packt Open Source

In 2010, Packt launched two new brands, Packt Open Source and Packt Enterprise, in order to continue its focus on specialization. This book is part of the Packt Open Source brand, home to books published on software built around Open Source licences, and offering information to anybody from advanced developers to budding web designers. The Open Source brand also runs Packt's Open Source Royalty Scheme, by which Packt gives a royalty to each Open Source project about whose software a book is sold.

Writing for Packt

We welcome all inquiries from people who are interested in authoring. Book proposals should be sent to author@packtpub.com. If your book idea is still at an early stage and you would like to discuss it first before writing a formal book proposal, contact us; one of our commissioning editors will get in touch with you.

We're not just looking for published authors; if you have strong technical skills but no writing experience, our experienced editors can help you develop a writing career, or simply get some additional reward for your expertise.

Learning Ext JS

ISBN: 978-1-847195-14-2   Paperback: 324 pages

Build dynamic, desktop-style user interfaces for your data-driven web applications

1. Learn to build consistent, attractive web interfaces with the framework components

2. Integrate your existing data and web services with Ext JS data support

3. Enhance your JavaScript skills by using Ext's DOM and AJAX helpers

4. Extend Ext JS through custom components

Learning jQuery

ISBN: 978-1-847192-50-9   Paperback: 380 pages

Better Interaction Design and Web Development with Simple JavaScript Techniques

1. Create better, cross-platform JavaScript code

2. Learn detailed solutions to specific client-side problems

3. For web designers who want to create interactive elements for their designs

4. For developers who want to create the best user interface for their web applications

open source
community experience distilled

PACKT PUBLISHING

jQuery 1.4 Reference Guide

A comprehensive exploration of the popular JavaScript library

Karl Swedberg Jonathan Chaffer

jQuery 1.4 Reference Guide

ISBN: 978-1-849510-04-2   Paperback: 336 pages

This book and eBook is a comprehensive exploration of the popular JavaScript library

1. Quickly look up features of the jQuery library

2. Step through each function, method, and selector expression in the jQuery library with an easy-to-follow approach

3. Understand the anatomy of a jQuery script

4. Write your own plug-ins using jQuery's powerful plug-in architecture

JavaFX 1.2
Application Development Cookbook

Over 60 recipes to create rich Internet applications with many exciting features

Vladimir Vivien

JavaFX 1.2 Application Development Cookbook

ISBN: 978-1-847198-94-5   Paperback: 332 pages

Over 60 recipes to create rich Internet applications with many exciting features

1. Easily develop feature-rich internet applications to interact with the user using various built-in components of JavaFX

2. Enhance the look and feel of your application by embedding multimedia components such as images, audio, and video

4. Part of Packt's Cookbook series: Each recipe is a carefully organized sequence of instructions to complete the task as efficiently as possible

Please check **www.PacktPub.com** for information on our titles

CPSIA information can be obtained at www.ICGtesting.com
Printed in the USA
268649BV00004BA/19/P